The
John Hannam Interviews
The Wight Connections

The
John Hannam Interviews
The Wight Connections

The revealing stories behind John's
memorable interviews with past and
present Isle of Wight people

This book is dedicated to my parents, Roy and Ena Hannam

John's Mum and Dad, Roy and Ena Hannam

Personal thanks to those who have always given me so much support.

My late wife, Heather, Sean and Caroline, Celia and John Vosper, Diane and Peter Eames, Paul and Shauna Shutler and my partner, Roberta Crismass. I would also like to thank many close friends for their belief in me.

Grateful thanks to the *Isle of Wight County Press* for the use of so many of their photographs.

First published 2018 by John Hannam. Copyright © John Hannam

Book design by Mike Lambert, Freshwater, Isle of Wight PO40 9PP

Printed by Short Run Press Limited
25 Bittern Road, Sowton Industrial Estate, Exeter, Devon EX2 7LW

ISBN 978-0-9504126-6-5

ALSO AVAILABLE are John Hannam's books recalling his interviews with pop stars from the '50s, '60s and '70s and those with the stars of stage and screen past and present.

Contents

John Hannam

John with Johnny Vincent

BACK IN 1974 when John began interviewing local and famous people, as a freelance journalist and broadcaster, he made a policy that he would only undertake in-person interviews. Over the years this may have lost him a few huge names but he has bravely stuck to his principals. For John, actually meeting his guests is of paramount importance. Even in his many years as a showbusiness feature writer he has always applied the same rule.

John thrives on doing hours of research for many interviews and has a friendly technique, which has been praised by many people over the past 44 years. Many have gone out of their way to congratulate him. John also prides himself on being a member of the old school of chat show hosts. He's had no desire to be the star of the show or to use his guests as pure fodder for cheap laughs. Private lives have never been on his agenda and his interviewees have always trusted him profusely. So much so, that on occasions, they have just opened up to reveal unexpected stories.

John has gained such a high reputation within the entertainment industry and Radio 2 have used around 20 of his archive recordings for their national radio shows. His archive is rated as one of the best in the British Isles. With over 5000 interviews to his name, including hundreds of Islanders, it's easy to see why.

A few years ago John decided to issue three CDs containing extracts from his many interviews. One featured past showbiz legends and the other two contained some of the Isle of Wight's best-loved characters. All three have now sold out.

This book features the stories behind over 100 of his acclaimed interviews with local people and he reveals memorable moments with Bill Brett, Sylvia Jones, Morris Barton, Henry Adams, Celia Imrie, Alby Payne, Kenneth Kendall and many others.

Luckily, over 44 years, John has made many friends, some famous and others just delightful local Islanders. He just loves people and has built up a reputation of being fully trustworthy and a perfect professional.

John with Stephanie Slater

John's new and archive interviews can be heard all over the world on regular new online podcasts. Links can be obtained from John's website www.johnhannam.com plus the Isle of Wight Radio website, Spotify, iTunes and others.

Foreword by Craig Douglas

I WANT TO TELL YOU a little story. I used to play football at school for Barton Boys and the first time I ever saw John Hannam, he was wearing a yellow jersey and in goal for East Cowes Grange Road School. After the game he complained of a bad back, as we'd hit six goals past him. I've never let him forget that I actually scored three of them.

I will say, he can now hold a microphone much better than he could a football. He's been doing it for many years and has interviewed so many stars.

Craig with Heather Hannam

In the early days of my career, John wrote all the latest news about my records, TV shows and concerts for the *County Press*. He also wrote letters about me to the national pop newspapers and magazines. I was so grateful for this. In 1959, I invited him to the Commodore Cinema, Ryde, to meet me, before one of my Sunday shows there. We've been great mates ever since. John and his lovely wife, Heather, travelled all around Britain to see me perform.

Craig and Priness Anne

They came to Edinburgh, Weston-Super-Mare, Southend, Portsmouth, Cardiff and the London Palladium. I know he's always been thrilled by the success of Islanders and has helped them all he can.

Having been born in Newport, I am excited by this book, which features many Islanders, including my old Pan Estate next door neighbour, Morris Barton, and

Craig and John

Craig Douglas

my good friend Mike Reader. I wish John a lot of success with it and many more interviews in the future. Good luck, mate.

Craig Douglas

Introduction

John Hannam

I WAS BORN IN EAST COWES and have had a love for Island people since I first started school. I always had great support and encouragement from my parents, Roy and Ena. Outside of the family, some of my earliest influences were school teachers like Miss Thompson, Mrs Weeks and Bill Read. There were also Sunday school teachers including Miss Hollis, Mrs Dowden, Mrs Templeton, Stan Guttridge, Bern Jeffries, Den Brewin and Jim Walkinshaw. Later, at Cowes Secondary Modern, Vic Reid and Bill Capps encouraged my interest in sport. Teachers like Roy Templeton and Humphrey Matthews always showed a real interest in my education.

East Cowes town councillors Sinclair Glossop and Jim Moon were local guys who really impressed me. The local East Cowes Vics players like Joe Reed, Mike Gallagher, Scotty Yule and Roy Pridmore were all early heroes of mine. When I went to my first job, at Newport mineral water manufacturers Gould, Hibberd and Randall, Leslie Harvey, who has a chapter in this book, and Bob Dubber influenced the shape of my life to come. Later, when I joined United Biscuits, Bert Spicer was a real diamond.

I'd always heard local East Cowes stories of the town's Les Maskell, who went on to play football for Norwich City. I was so excited when the Island's Roy Shiner was scoring goals for Sheffield Wednesday. I was also in awe of JB Priestley, who lived at Brook. I once saw him on a Southampton ferry. Uffa Fox was another icon for me and my mother had some great stories about him. Then there was Cowes-born Cliff Michelmore, a radio and TV personality. In 1958, Terry Perkins, a local Newport milkman, found fame as pop star Craig Douglas. I was so motivated by the success of Islanders. When I became a small part of the local media, I was determined to track down some very famous locals. Hence, I interviewed Brian Murphy, Jeremy Irons, Sheila Hancock, Marius Goring, Phill Jupitus, Mark King and Snowy White.

John winning the Hampshire Boys' Mile

During my life I have met so many unforgettable Isle of Wight characters and many are in this book. We will never again see the likes of Sylvia Jones, Fred Price, Dave Death, Den Phillips and Tony Best. It's such a real pleasure to relive memories of the fun I had with them.

I've always had an ambition to write a book about Island people. *The John Hannam Interviews, The Wight Connections*, has made this dream feasible. I have also included some famous names, who, over the years, have made the Island their home. People like Celia Imrie, Kenneth Kendall, Michael Sheard, Dick Taylor and Alan Titchmarsh.

My media mentor was the late Keith Newbery. I owe everything I have ever achieved, to him. He gave me my first real chance and opened quite a few doors for me.

I have admiration for every single person in this book. I've been so proud and privileged to have met them all. I am also thrilled that Craig Douglas has written the foreword.

John Hannam

CHAPTER 1

Sylvia Jones

Back in 1994 I was in the Brighstone Spar stores and the owner David Hollis, a regular listener to my IW Radio chat show, suggested a perfect guest for my live programme. It was the Military Road farmer Sylvia Jones. I met up with her and within two minutes realised he was spot on. Amazingly, in the 26 years of the show the two guests who created the biggest response were Cliff Richard and Sylvia.

We met at Sutton Farm a day or two before her live appearance and I had a job to wait until the Sunday lunchtime. Sylv had also written out her greatest stories on a piece of old cardboard and it was far better than some television comedy scripts. During her radio debut appearance, at the age of 74, we had phone calls from all along the south coast of England.

A few times during that first-ever radio appearance she asked me: "Can I say this on the radio?" Her stories became legendary and I'm still asked about 'that old lady from the Military Road.' Obviously, she came several times by public demand.

Sylv and I became close friends. Wherever we met she was always wearing her old brown smock tied up with string. That was the least of my worries. Her instant greeting was always a full-on hard kiss on the lips.

There were so many wartime stories and she vividly remembered seeing the German planes flying under the electricity cable lines and having to dodge the bullets, as they shot at anything that moved. They also bartered with the American troops stationed opposite their farm at the Atherfield Holiday Camp.

Due to a shortage of local labour, her father, rather reluctantly, took some German prisoners of war to work on the farm. I'll never forget the way she told it.

"We'd never seen a foreigner before and when the truck arrived and they got down I thought they look like us. We gave them a meal and they ate like us. They couldn't speak English and we couldn't speak German, so we understood each other with sign language."

I never tired of the story about the late night courting couple. With her true Isle of Wight accent it became a gem, no matter how many times you'd heard it.

"I was driving the tractor down our back lane late one night and there was a car parked in the way. The car was all misted up but I had to knock on the window. When they opened the door they didn't have many clothes on. I said I was sorry to stop them and I hoped they could get steam up again."

James Mason made a movie on their farm in the late '30s called I Met A Murderer. They used her father's Ford V8 as the police car and their caravan was involved in the story. The climax of the movie was shot at Whale Chine.

In Sylvia's early days it was a real treat just to go into Newport on a bus. She had a three mile walk to school at Shorwell and the same to get home. No wonder she was so slim. Later in life she went abroad three times – and there was a story behind that adventure.

"The first time I went I didn't take a case full of clothes because I took all my own grub. I didn't fancy all that oily stuff over there."

We did a video together at Sutton Farm and it became a best seller in Brighstone – and far beyond. Sadly, Sylvia died in 2000 and I think of her every time I drive along the Military Road.

CHAPTER 2

Cliff Michelmore

FOR MANY OF US of a certain age, the first famous Islander we ever heard about was Cliff Michelmore. Not far off 20 million tuned in every Sunday lunchtime to hear *Two Way Family Favourites*, hosted by Cliff and his wife, Jean Metcalfe. Then he fronted huge BBC television shows like *Panorama*, *Tonight*, *24 Hours* and *Holiday*.

My mother-in-law, Peggy Greenham, was so proud of the fact that she went to school with Cliff. I can still remember the first time I ever saw him. It was at a match to celebrate the opening of the JS Whites cricket ground, where Hampshire went on to play a few county games. I had my autograph book handy and they were delighted to sign. There was certainly a buzz when they walked around the ground.

The next time I saw them in person was on October 12, 1963. Heather and I had got married and when we got to the end of Ryde Pier, heading for London, Cliff and Jean, who had been to an Island family wedding, were there to see the happy couple off on their honeymoon.

In 1998, to celebrate Isle of Wight Radio going to FM, I decided Cliff would be just the right guest to have on my show – and so it proved. Heather and I went to their home near Petersfield and were made welcome. There were a couple of embarrassing moments. Jean did not want to come on the interview or even be in the room while we recorded it. We could hear an exchange of words, from our hosts, in another room. When I began the recording, I made a false start and had to go again. I probably tried too hard when confronted by such a media icon. Any early nerves were quickly forgotten and we talked for over an hour. In the end, he seemed to be impressed. I never found out for 18 years that he really was and had also appreciated my research. This came via June Butchers, a family member from Cowes, who actually set up the interview.

Cliff loved the Island and they had a house in Bembridge for many years and often joined in local village events. He'd also enjoyed his school days at Cowes Denmark Road.

"Two teachers there had such an influence on my life. These were Mr Guppy, the headmaster, and Mr Waller. They became father figures in my life and I went to them for advice."

Cliff's family had moved to the Island from Devon because his father had TB. Our Island air was deemed healthier and the Ventnor Sanatorium was close at hand. Cliff was born here but his father died when he was just two. Six years later his mother died and he was brought up by relatives, Joe and Vi Butchers, at Baskett's Farm, Gurnard.

"It proved such a happy time for me. I just loved it and did my homework sat by the nearby pond. I also remember reading my first book there, *Scott Of The Antarctic*," reflected Cliff.

I'll never forget that interview at Petersfield. I quickly sensed he was blissfully unaware of his popularity. To him, it was just a job and he did the best he could. There was not a hint of any ego or self importance. Despite knowing there were millions watching him on live television, he never got flustered. The only occasion he was nervous was when he fronted his first General Election results programme. There was extra pressure because it was the first one after the death of the legendary Richard Dimbleby.

Our Cliff had a great life and his story included Gene Kelly, the Beatles, Roger Moore, Sophia Loren and Louis Armstrong. Not bad for a kid from Denmark Road!

CHAPTER 3

Johnny Vincent

IN THE '50s a Wootton teenager leisurely progressed from singing John Wesley hymns to the latest hits from Frankie Laine. Then young John Mowbray suddenly discovered rock 'n' roll. Virtually overnight he became Johnny Vincent and was mobbed at local gigs – especially when he sang *Blue Suede Shoes*. I met him 30 years later and he was still rockin' – but then as a grandad.

I have a programme from week commencing February 3, 1958, when Johnny and another Island singer, Terry Perkins, appeared on a variety bill at the Empire Theatre, Portsmouth, topped by Maxine Daniels. Also on that bill were the Island's *Nomads Skiffle Group*. With rock 'n' roll so popular it seemed Johnny would go on to become a star. In fact, it was young ballad singer Perkins, whose name was changed to Craig Douglas, who went on to world fame.

Back in 1986, I set out to find Johnny Vincent for my *Weekly Post Stage Talk* column. After an unsuccessful six months, I had quite a shock one day when the milkman knocked my door for his money. He asked if it was true I was looking for his dad, Johnny Vincent. I never realised my milkman's surname was actually Mowbray. Within a week or two I was with his dad in Andover. He'd left the Island in 1965.

In 1955 Commander Fulljames spotted Johnny's potential and booked him for his Lakeside Club, at Wootton Creek. At that time he was singing Frankie Laine songs.

Johnny remembered it well. "When I first got up to sing at Lakeside, I was so nervous I had my back to the audience. They had a blind pianist there called Pete Unwin who could play anything, including the new Jerry Lee Lewis style." This was perfect for the birth of Johnny Vincent, as a rock 'n' roll singer.

Wherever Johnny went on the Island he was asked to sing a song. It would normally be *Blue Suede Shoes*, with any group that could back him. Then he had his own group, the *Alley Cats*.

Johnny quickly became a local cult figure with his pink jacket, black shirt and luminous coloured socks. The same fans flocked to all his gigs and the local bikers kind of adopted him. He was mobbed wherever he went. Sometimes he arrived for a gig on the back of Dave Pritchett's Triumph 500. He yearned for his own Cadillac but only managed a Hudson Terraplane, with his own chauffeur.

Robin Britten, the Island cinema owner who discovered Craig Douglas, had equally big plans for Johnny.

"He put me in a stiff brown suit and I just couldn't move. Then he wanted me to take elocution lessons and all that stuff. I did make a demo record at London's EMI Studio. Robin was keen to change my image, seek original songs and give me a new name.

"I didn't want that. I only did it because I enjoyed it and was just happy for my mates to come along and have a good time."

On one memorable occasion when Johnny was singing at Sandown's Copacabana Club, Tommy Steele popped in. He used to come to the Island on secret visits and camp in our forests. Johnny even told me he took him to his auntie's for a cup of tea.

One of Johnny's greatest fans was a young lad called Les Payne, also featured in this book. Many years later he wrote a song called So Long and it mentioned a singer called Johnny Ringo, alias Johnny Vincent.

CHAPTER 4

Julie Clifton

AT ONE TIME Julie Clifton was the most photographed person on the Isle of Wight. Apparently, during her younger days she had briefly been a model but this had nothing to do with a catwalk, the Planet Fashion Collection or Barney's Roadhouse. She was the public face of the Earl Mountbatten Hospice for many years and attended so many local functions to collect cheques and promote their fundraising.

Back in the '70s Julie was in the fashion business and she launched and designed the Planet Collection for Windsmoor. Perhaps, I shouldn't say she was inspired by the cut out dolls-to-dress featured in the *Bunty* magazine. In reality, that led, eventually, to her setting up 32 Planet franchise units within famous stores like Selfridges and Harrods.

Julie, a lady of admirable principals, once told me the reason she resigned from Windsmoor. "I was called into the office and asked if I was interviewing for the Harlem Globetrotters? They told me we do not employ black girls in our shops and so I left."

Yves Saint Laurent in Paris got wind of her availability and she became their UK marketing director. She modified their fashions for the British market and even appeared in magazines, although, she claims never as a model. I'm not so sure.

When Julie became pregnant, her husband, Paul, wanted their child to be raised and educated on the Island. Hence they moved here and she gave up the fashion business. It worked out so well. Their son, Tom, is now an airline pilot who flies all over the world.

Over the years I've enjoyed some great moments of fun with Julie. She's always been a lady who could light up a room as soon as she walked through the door, often looking like a million dollars. That special laugh has also always given her away.

Many will remember her days as the owner of Barney's Roadhouse. She once told me, during one of our many interviews: "I could write a book on those days, particularly about the car park fights, even before they'd got into the disco. People came from all over the Island and I was just happy to be a barmaid."

A marriage breakdown eventually led Julie to voluntary work at the EM Hospice, inspired by her affection for Barbara Whitewood. She stayed 18 years and during this time, in her role as fundraiser, millions of pounds were donated. She was also in at the beginning of Walk the Wight and later negotiated with Moreys to keep the event going. When she eventually resigned, so many people were surprised.

"I loved the job and the volunteers but it just wasn't right for me at that particular time. Therefore, I decided to move on."

Julie was also keen to praise the work of a later EM Hospice fundraiser, Karen Eales, another gem of a lady.

In more recent years Julie has worked for other local charities. During one of our interviews, she was working for Age UK, formerly Age Concern. I left her home in a buoyant mood, following coffee, cake and a great chat. On arriving home I found just one letter on my doormat. It was from, would you believe, Age UK. Then my exhilaration suddenly ended. It was about funeral planning!

Tom, her airline pilot son, invited me to spend an hour or so at a land-based Airbus cockpit simulator. I managed to bring on every cabin warning light before I crashed. Apparently, I failed the test!

CHAPTER 5
David Gurd

"LOOK OUT, Gurdy's about!" That was a familiar warning from Island motorists and bikers from 1964 to the mid '80s – and most times a few more descriptive words were added. David Gurd was the Island's most notorious copper and could arrive from nowhere on his powerful motorbike. You could never see his eyes because of those mirrored lens sun glasses – but you knew it was him. I don't think Dave was particularly religious but he always came out of the small chapel in Clatterford Road, to catch a flying biker.

I kept in touch with Dave after he left the Island and the last time I saw him, as ever, we had great fun at his Dorset home. I actually took a bus from Lymington, just in case he'd come out of retirement!

Contrary to general belief, he did not book his own grandmother but he did set up his lovely wife Pat in a Yarmouth speed trap. A few days before I arrived he'd received his first-ever speeding ticket. Initially, when the boot was on the other foot, he was far from happy. He scrutinised the date and realised it was on a day when he didn't drive because of the medication he was on.

"I quickly handed over the paperwork to the guilty driver – my wife Pat. She was doing 36mph," said a relieved Gurdy.

I'll never forget the day I asked this lovely lady who worked in Chale Stores and often made me a cup of tea, when I was a salesman for United Biscuits, what her surname was. When she replied "Gurd" I must have looked startled. She quickly added: "Yes, I'm his wife."

Dave had so many stories to relate and made two appearances on my radio chat show. On one occasion his daughter had to go to Cowes to play badminton and dad decided to wait in the Painters Arms pub. He was not recognised by the talk-a-holic sat at the bar and the friendly guy even bought him a drink. For some reason the subject got around to that much maligned Island speed cop David Gurd. Guess who joined in? Just as he was about to leave the guy asked Dave what his name was. Apparently, it was a moment to savour. He told him, wished him good night and added "I hope we meet again."

In 1976 when Jim Davidson appeared at the Ponda Rosa, Ryde, as the Saturday night dinner dance cabaret star, he was doing all that "nick nick" police routine. I asked Dave if he would make a mock arrest of Jim to make a great picture for the *Weekly Post*. Of course, he was up for it but the chief of police would not allow it.

Was Dave's reputation exaggerated? He said it was, of course.

"Actually I let off more people than I booked but if drivers got aggressive, after a warning, I would book them. I never took action on people doing under 35mph."

Escorting the Royals was always a thrill for him and he remembered Lord Louis Mountbatten with particular pleasure. He had to get used to 'Mountbatten time.' Once Dave was told off for arriving 30 seconds late for a function in Lake.

David Gurd was much admired by his police colleagues. I was privileged to go to his funeral in Dorset and it was so emotional. The hearse followed a police motorbike rider with his blue light flashing.

CHAPTER 6

Anthony Minghella

WHEN ANTHONY Minghella was growing up in his parents cafe in Ryde, he used to take advantage of the fact that the Commodore Cinema was just in the road behind and the projectionist, Vernon Cook, allowed him to come into the box to see the movies. He was particularly inspired by the films of Italian director Franco Zeffirelli. No-one could have imagined that years later Anthony would make an Oscar-winning acceptance speech in Hollywood.

I knew the Minghella family well and remember seeing Anthony in the cafe, doing his homework or helping out. Like many Islanders, I often bought a cornet and flake from his ice cream van.

I vividly remember the first time he came live into my Sunday lunchtime radio show. He'd made me laugh just before the red light came on and as the theme played I introduced the show as 'John Hannam Wheets'. With that, Anthony burst out laughing and repeated my mistake. We had fun for the next hour.

Heather came in with me and sat with Anthony's dad, Eddie, as studio guests. Ever the great salesman, Eddie whispered to her: "He's not mentioning the ice cream enough." Five years later Anthony plugged the ice cream in front of millions of viewers all around the world, when he won the Best Director Oscar for *The English Patient*.

During our 1992 interview, Anthony found it rather strange that he was back on the Island to present awards at his old school, Sandown Grammar, then renamed as Sandown High.

"It was somewhat ironic that one of the world's worst students should have gone back to give out prizes at his old school."

As a teenager he played in various local pop groups. This was purely to get way from his father's ice cream business and help him forget about school work.

Actually, he did love those days in the Ryde cafe.

"It was a wonderful experience and from an early age it meant I got used to meeting a lot of people. Sharing our family kitchen with the cafe's meant all my trials and tribulations were lived out in public. Bad school reports, soccer defeats and broken romances were all shared among egg and chips, ice creams and dirty plates."

He did admit in his book about *Truly, Madly, Deeply*, his first major movie, that, in the end, he was desperate to get away. It was no surprise when he went off to Hull University.

I admired Anthony so much. The Minghella family have always been so close and have enjoyed each others successes. During his early days in movies he had faith in his own personal band of actors. Hence, he used Juliet Stevenson, Alan Rickman and Jude Law, among others. The Island's Graeme Du-Fresne and Mike Jolliffe, his local pop group mates, were also great early influences. Graeme, also an actor, played a ghost in *Truly, Madly, Deeply*.

Anthony went out of his way to help. Sometimes he would manage to squeeze in an interview with me during an Island premiere. Once, I was invited to a favourite cinema of his, in Hampstead, where he lived, to do an interview.

The very last time I actually met him was on a Saturday morning visit to the family home in Ryde. We talked about his career and latest movie, *Breaking And Entering*. I stayed to lunch and then he was off to Fratton Park to watch his beloved Pompey. The first thing he did every morning, anywhere in the world, was to check the Portsmouth Football Club website.

It's still so hard to believe he left us in 2008. There would have been more great movies to come.

CHAPTER 7

Crisco

BRADLEY WALSH, Joe Pasquale and Shane Richie have all become huge stars in recent years. Amazingly, they were all influenced by Island entertainer Crisco, real name Chris Cox. They were all resident holiday centre entertainers and one of their regular visiting cabaret acts was Crisco and they always watched him from the wings. Whenever I interview any of them, they always ask how he is. The trio learned so much from him.

I have met barmen who have worked in a holiday centre or hotel for years and they had never tired of Crisco, on his regular weekly visits. I once booked Chris for an Isle of Wight Amateur Theatre Awards presentation night. Many of the Island's young burgeoning performers had never seen an act like it before. Sadly, it was a sign of the times. They loved his zany humour, crazy dancing and brilliant comedy magic. They just gazed in wonder, as he produced so many razor blades from his mouth and playing cards from thin air. He came back the next year and stormed them again.

We've all heard stories of entertainers who should have been stars but never made it. In Crisco's case, it was the real truth. With a fan club of Walsh, Pasquale and Richie to back him up, it just should have happened.

I think sometimes Chris was too worried about upsetting local hoteliers. He often did three gigs or more in the same night. At one time he was doing 31 Island shows a week. He should have headed for the mainland and not worried about local kids parties and small hotels. He had the opportunities but didn't always take them.

I asked him if he regretted not becoming a household name.

"I can't help but think about it. My wife often reminds me of the opportunities I missed. Twice I had famous agents wanting to sign me up and if I'd gone with a top management company things might have been different.

"Once I was in a Welsh agent's office and she had a call from the producer of Hughie Green's *Opportunity Knocks*. They were looking for a comedy speciality act but I said I was too busy with bookings and could not get to the studio."

When Michael Barrymore was at the top of his game he was also a Crisco fan and he booked him to perform at his star-studded house parties. Other stars who were also among his admirers were Max Wall, Freddie Starr and Dick Emery.

Since 1960, Chris has performed over 23,000 gigs. He has made a few top television shows, including *The Wayne Dobson Show.*

Chris has always courted publicity and the story of how his wife cooked his pet rabbit, which it stated appeared in his act, went all around the world. It was not true, by the way. It was a local reporter's fake news story. It led to hundreds of radio and TV shows. On another occasion, there were huge headlines when Mary Whitehouse walked out of his show, at a Blackpool Conservative Conference.

He's worked on pop concerts with The Who, Slade and the Bee Gees. Talking of pop stars, he once appeared on an Irish TV show and turned down the chance to go out for a drink with the group who were also on the show. He'd never heard of Queen or Freddie Mercury.

He also prides himself on looking old for the last 40 years – which suits his act perfectly.

I was a fan from the first time I saw him work.

CHAPTER 8

Bob and Pam Everson

IT SEEMED FATE when Totland's Bob and Pam Everson finally got married. They lived next door to each other in Brading and never realised it, although she was only eight at the time and he was so much older, probably in his teens, and still had hair. Years later he drove her wedding day car, was smitten by the bride and even tried to tempt her to forget the ceremony and run away with him. All he got was a filthy look. At that precise moment, she would never have dreamed that one day they would actually get married and run a funeral directors business.

Both came from different backgrounds but the contrast in their individual skills and personalities has made them just perfect for a business that would be beyond the capabilities of many people. They founded their company in 1990.

Bob had early dreams of becoming a movie star. He was never going to be the prototype for John Travolta but was unbeatable at the twist and even got banned from the Sandown Pier Ballroom for winning too many times. His brother, Mick, was a great influence. He was a popular local rock 'n' roll singer but young Bob was too shy to emulate him. Later in life he managed to acquire a lot more confidence and has proved a hit in many West Wight productions.

During one of our interviews he told me: "My attitude to life changed when I started to play golf. I discovered many things about myself. You have no one else to rely on and I worked hard at improving. Up until then, if I couldn't do things well, I tended to give up."

Pam dreamed of becoming a nanny in a posh country house. There was no *Downton Abbey* on the horizon. Her father had other ideas and filled in her application form for the Nat West Bank and drove her to the interview.

If Bob had not bought an old London taxi they might never have met. That's how he drove her wedding car. This work also meant he attended funerals which eventually led to Newport's Hamilton and Marshall and Twymans at Freshwater.

"When the big boys came to the Island to take over some of our established funeral businesses, I just didn't like their methods and ethics. I had my own ideas and could see how to make improvements," said Bob.

By this time, Bob and Pam were together, having finally met, properly, after her marriage dissolved. Amazingly, Bob got to know Pam's mother and daughter long before he met her – other than that short brusque meeting in her wedding car.

Undertakers need a sense of humour. When my partner, Roberta, can't make it, I sometimes take Pam to a Mayflower Theatre press night. I'll never forget the first two.

Early on in the musical *Spamalot* there's a scene where they say "throw your dead bodies up here on the cart." I remember whispering to her that this was a bit close to home. Our next show together was the Peter James thriller *Dead Simple*, which was all about a guy being buried alive in a coffin. Again, we both saw the funny side.

Bob and Pam enjoy working together on stage and I love their own take on the Fiona and Charles characters from *Round The Horne*. Oh! Fiona – Oh! Charles – and all that stuff. Pam has played a few lady-of-the-night roles, of which I never cease to remind her.

They are both delighted that their son, Bertie, is now a part of the business. He's another exceptionally talented stage performer.

CHAPTER 9

Brian Murphy

DURING MY 44 years as an interviewer I have tried to track down as many Island-born stars as I can. These have included Jeremy Irons, Sheila Hancock, Phill Jupitus, Craig Douglas, Marius Goring, Mark King, Snowy White and, of course, Brian Murphy, also known by millions as a certain George Roper.

I took a rare holiday in 1976 and spent a few days in Bournemouth. I must admit, I did know Brian Murphy was starring in a summer season at the Pier Theatre and I managed to hide my cassette recorder in the boot. My devious plan had worked – and I'm sure Heather knew all along. In later years, to get me off the Island for a few days, she suggested I did a few interviews at the same time.

Brian was born in Ventnor and has always been very proud of that fact. His childhood memories went back to seeing top class professional repertory at the Town Hall Theatre.

"The first play I ever saw there was a comedy and I can still remember one particular actor, who made such an impression on me. Nowadays he would be accused of over-acting," said Brian.

His other great Island memory was our steam trains. "They always said those lovely old steam trains went so slowly you could almost pick bluebells from the carriage windows. I will never forget that steep hill up to Ventnor Town Station."

In more recent years Brian came back, with his wife Linda Regan, who was in the hit series Hi-de-Hi, for an evening at Newport's Apollo Theatre. I was honoured to be a part of it and interviewed him live on stage. The theatre had the set for their latest play in position – and he made the most of it.

The day before the gig we had a meal at the Buddle Inn, Niton, and, as expected, everybody recognised Brian. At one time, he'd also had grandparents in Ventnor and an aunt in St Helens.

With due respect to his early career, it was playing George Roper in Man About The House that changed Brian's life. Both he and Yootha Joyce, as his long suffering wife, were so popular they were given their own series, George and Mildred. This went on to be even more successful than the original show they were featured in. It topped the viewing charts for so many weeks.

Such was the show's impact, many thought Brian and Yootha were married. Both of them were virtually mobbed in public and could not safely go into pubs. Sadly, just before their final series was due to be filmed, Yootha became seriously ill and subsequently died. She was at the peak of her career.

Brian continued to be in constant demand and went on to make the classic trilogy of TV's The Booze Cruise. The third episode is one of the funniest shows I have ever seen on television. It's better than any bottled tonic. Then came Last Of The Summer Wine.

I once had a brilliant day at Brian's home in Bromley and indoors he was not unlike one or two characters he'd played. Delightful company. I even managed to persuade him to put his name to an Isle of Wight Amateur Theatre Awards trophy. It became The Brian Murphy Best Newcomer Of The Year Award.

In 2017 I attended the Renown Pictures Film Festival in Rickmansworth and Brian was one of the star guests. This was organised by the fabulous Talking Pictures TV channel. We had a quick chat but he was busy on stage and signing autographs for fans.

CHAPTER 10

Lee Probert

WHENEVER I see Lee Probert, the Island's Premiership football referee, on a televised match, my mind always goes back to Niton's cliff top pitch and a story he told me on the first occasion we ever met. Lee's parents, who always gave him great support and encouragement, also shared the secret.

One Saturday morning, he was told, unofficially, by local appointments secretary, Andy King, that they had no referee at Niton for that afternoon. He hinted that it might be an idea if his parents took him out for a drive and made sure they went by the ground. It worked like a dream – and despite being only 15, a year short of the required age, he did take charge of the match. From Niton to Wembley Stadium, as a FA Cup Final referee, was an amazing journey. I bet his mother, Sharon, remembered that Niton visit, when she was sat in the stands. His late father, Tom, would have been so proud.

I love turning on a match a wee bit late, to avoid all the pre-match pundits, and recognising Lee's running style. He's quicker than I imagined. I found that out the last time we met.

We were due to chat in Shanklin but Lee rang to ask if we could meet at the Fairway Sports Complex. He was due a training session and would I like to join him. I ran my first 800 metres for 40 years and couldn't keep up with him. I was careful not to tell him my age. I did admit that in the late '50s I could run one in about 2 minutes 15 seconds. In this one, Lee timed me at four minutes 10 seconds. It couldn't have been age, surely. I did have a pacemaker, sewn into my chest, and his heart monitor wasn't working.

As usual, I needed to get permission from the Football Association to talk to Lee. Luckily, they knew my style and did not have a problem with it. I knew he was not allowed to talk about incidents in a game or individual players or managers.

I did remember seeing Lee in a Newcastle v Manchester United match and he made a remark to Wayne Rooney, which the Reds star really laughed at. He does enjoy having a good rapport with many of the players and it must help the spirit of the game.

From those humble beginnings in Niton, Lee has gone on to referee in Japan, Spain, Holland, Russia and Germany.

"The Stoke v Manchester City 2011 Cup Final, when I was the fourth official, was a special moment for me. There were 90,000 people there.

"My long term friend from schooldays, Adrian Hall-Wilson, who was going to the match, got in touch to see how we could get back to Sandown's Ferncliff Gardens, to relive the final, score the goals and be the star players, as we used to do. I had to tell him I wouldn't be able to make it," said Lee, who went even better three years later.

He refereed the 2014 Cup Final between Arsenal and Hull City. This superseded any previous highlights and is one of the greatest accolades you can obtain in English football. Sadly, he missed the whole of the 2015/16 season because of a back injury. His career was threatened but Harley Street thought otherwise.

Lee and James Linington, another top referee, who also began his career locally, have proved that Island boys, if they start young enough, can reach the top.

When Lee qualified for the National League, back in the early '90s, he was not too keen to be seen on television. That quickly changed. Rumour has it, there's now even an Island beach hut named after him.

CHAPTER 11

Jim Blake

IT WAS ALWAYS such a job to even get Jim Blake off his beloved Ventnor beach. He did sometimes cross the road at lunchtime to enjoy a quick pint at a nearby pub. In the summer of 2004, when I last met up with him, he'd just celebrated 60 years as a longshoreman. It was something of a record summer for him – and it had nothing to do with deck chairs. He'd actually been to Newport three times.

Jim's ancestors were shipwrecked on Bembridge Ledge, en route from Ireland, back in the late 1700s. It was quite possible they had no plans to even visit the Island. In the end, they settled at the villages of Steephill and Flowers Brook. In 1830, Jim's great grandfather, James, established the family business on Ventnor seafront.

I loved talking to Jim and could listen to his memories for hours – and he never took his cap off.

As a schoolboy, he could remember being sent to collect deck chair money from Emperor Haile Selassie, then in exile, who was staying at the Beach Hotel. On another occasion he picked up a Cadbury family heiress from a moored boat. She was suffering from a bout of seasickness and recovered at an nearby hotel.

He recalled how the beach was closed with barbed wire, early tubular scaffolding and tank traps during the Second World War. There were also three concrete pillboxes on the seafront.

"I can remember the Home Guard practising in them. They would fire one round of shots and then march home," said Jim.

In 1947, at the age of 17, he actually went to London. There was a pea soup fog for a week and that put him off the mainland.

On August 8, 1948, there was a tremendous storm that caused so much damage. A local policeman helped by getting the street lights back on. They always went off at midnight. The plane crash, in February 1985, saw a lady lose her life. Jim also witnessed a few vehicles go off the sea wall and end up on the beach. One of which, was a milk lorry. On another occasion a yacht got caught in one of Blake's fishing nets, which proved so lucky for them, as they were heading for rocks at the time.

Hundreds of swimmers were saved, many after ignoring the warnings. Some wore old knitted bathing costumes that dragged them under.

He told me: "We used to watch swimmers through binoculars and sense they were going to be in trouble and put to sea before they shouted for help.

"In 60 years I've only known of three drownings and we couldn't help any of them. One had a heart attack, one dived in and hit the bottom and was never seen again and the other had ignored the red flag and was washed away in wild seas."

Jim, who was awarded the British Empire Medal in the early '80s, loved the days holidaymakers had no cars and the men were happy just to sit on the beach all day in their gabardine coats and trilbies. Hopefully, in Blake's deckchairs.

I love the story of the time Jim's wife, Rosemary, left him to it and went on holiday to Egypt. Her most frightening experience was being picked up by her husband from Shanklin Station. He drove the wrong way up a one-way street.

I couldn't resist asking him about the day a full beer barrel rolled off a lorry and on to the beach? Did the brewers get it back? He was non-committal but mentioned a few locals seemed to have headaches around that time.

CHAPTER 12

Stephanie Slater

THERE IS NO DOUBT that my most emotional live radio interview ever, came on Sunday March 28, 2004. My guest was Stephanie Slater and I was close to tears on several occasions. We'd met for the first time a few days earlier and all was set for the interview. I knew just how to put her in the right frame of mind. The show opened with a record from her favourite group, Big Country, and I could sense her excitement. Then I told her that we needed to go back to January 22, 1992, when her nightmare first began.

"I was showing a potential client called Michael Sams around a house in Birmingham and didn't realise he was a murderer, extortionist and kidnapper. He'd asked to go back upstairs to view something and then pushed me into the bathroom at knife point. He then gagged and blindfolded me, led me out through the garden and drove me to Newark. Then he put me in a coffin-like box in a wheelie bin for eight days, while he negotiated with my employers."

Amazingly, a week earlier, when she was showing another person around the same house, a lady from next door had asked her if she ever got frightened about showing strangers around a house.

Stephanie continued her story: "The night before, I was with my best friend and we were excited because we'd booked a holiday on the Isle of Wight. It was one of my favourite places. Little did I know that the next day would change my life."

It was a harrowing story and, initially, she never revealed he'd raped her on the first night in his workshop. She was actually blindfolded the whole of the eight days.

"One night I thought I was dying. It was so cold and I couldn't shiver anymore. I'd read about near death experiences and although I was blindfolded, on the right I saw a point of light. Then I saw the face of Christ and it was real and he was breathing. Suddenly, all the pain and strife just left me. The face of Christ I saw was very similar to a painting I'd seen in Godshill Church."

Stephanie then fell asleep and woke up listening to the voice of Jimmy Young on Radio 2. It was not quite her scene – and he didn't play any Big Country. That story had an unexpected ending. At the end of the court case, she was thrilled to receive a huge bouquet from Jimmy Young.

"One night I dreamt of Frankie Howerd and he told me I would be okay and that he would look after me, but he was going to die that year." In fact, Frankie did die in that same year of 1992.

Stephanie's story made world headlines and Sams got life imprisonment. The *Sun* newspaper obtained an exclusive story and offered Stephanie the chance to go anywhere in the world, to undertake the interviews. The reporting team and cameraman were anticipating an exciting and glamorous location.

"There was just one place I wanted to go. I chose the Isle of Wight and had two weeks in Shanklin."

Stephanie and her long-term friend moved here in 1993 and her parents followed three years later. It was not easy for her.

"I locked myself away for a while, drank too much and thought about suicide."

Thankfully, things got a lot better and eventually she became an inspirational speaker at various police events.

Sadly, the lovely Stephanie died in 2017.

CHAPTER 13

Kite

OH BROTHER! That was a day that was. On Friday February 4, 1977, I had my first major scoop in the *Isle of Wight Weekly Post*. Three good friends, Andy Skelton, Doug Watson and Tim Marshall were in a band called *Brother*, who played at Keats Inn, Shanklin. I had written about them before and even had a Christmas card from them from The Virgin Cave Club in Copenhagen. This time it was really hot news.

The following day, February 5, they were going to be seen on the legendary TV series *New Faces*. I was the only one to know this – until I shared it with thousands of *Weekly Post* readers. They were the first Islanders to ever appear on the show. I even got a gold star from the editor. This was a huge television show and watched by many more than Simon Cowell's later reincarnations.

Over 40 years on, it's still a remarkable achievement that Brother won their first heat and impressed the judges, Mickie Most, Lionel Blair, Alan Freeman and Shaw Taylor. Andy Skelton is a brilliant songwriter and his *You've Got The Power* was their chosen song. Many years after that first *New Faces* appearance, I had all three live on my radio show and managed to shock them when one of the original judges, Shaw Taylor, walked through the door to surprise them on air.

Mickie Most advised them, on the show, to change their name as there was another group called The Brothers, who were currently in the pop charts. The following week they had to go back to *New Faces* to perform in the All-Winners show, with their hastily arranged new name of Kite.

They had the glory of being the top group in the whole series and were just thrilled to make the Gala Final. They did earn a Decca record deal and tours at home and abroad. I have always felt they were let down by their management and should have gone on to lasting fame.

Pop music is such a tough world to exist in but Andy, Doug and Tim are a little different. They are all quality musicians and since the late '70s they've continued to be professional musicians and enjoyed very successful careers.

Andy, the Kite singer and guitarist, has taught music for many years and, at one time, was in five bands, playing many different types of music. He's made records, had his songs recorded by other artists and also formed one of the first Abba tribute bands, Fabba. He also enjoys playing locally with New Moon at their annual Lower Hyde gigs.

Tim, who played bass in Kite, spent around 30 years playing on cruise liners. He also played in the Johnny Wiltshire Showband for Sandown Pavilion summer seasons. More recently he's been seen in several local bands and playing for both Southsea pantomimes and Shanklin Theatre summer shows.

Drummer Doug Watson had the regular band at Warner's, Bembridge Coast, for many years and won the holiday company's best band of the year title, from all the bands at other centres. They were also so popular with visiting cabaret stars for their musical backing. He's also so well known for playing in local groups.

CHAPTER 14

Darren Mew

BACK IN 1980 when young Darren Mew made his world swimming pool debut his parents made sure he had arm bands. That was in the West Wight Swimming Pool – and he was only three months old. No one could have predicted that, a few years down the line, he would became one of Britain's top swimmers and could be seen on television winning breaststroke medals all around the world. Thousands of Islanders were cheering for him in the Olympics, World, European and Commonwealth Games.

Amazingly, his life has been involved with two islands. He proved to be our most successful swimmer of all time and was coached, locally, by Ann and Trevor Collins. Since 2015 he's been in the Cayman Islands, where he runs The Darren Mew Sports and Fitness company. He first moved there in 2011, to coach local swimmers, before setting up his own business.

When I first decided to have Darren live on my radio show I was told he would barely say a word and I would have a tough time. He was just the opposite and proved a very astute young man. He came back a few more times.

Darren reflected on those early West Wight beginnings: "At club nights, Ann noticed I had big hands and big feet and might be perfect for the breaststroke." Unbeknown to him, Trevor had quickly realised his potential and even thought he could become one of the best in Europe. What a shrewd observation that was. Within 10 years he'd won a bronze medal in the European Junior Championships.

Apparently, he played football for West Wight Youth and scored a brilliant goal from the halfway line and has always insisted he meant it. He was a defender and one of his pals described him as "awkward to get by." He would love to have played for Southampton but, wisely, stuck with swimming.

Away from the pool, Darren may have initially seemed rather shy but he had the confidence and self-belief to go to the mainland, with no hint of an inferiority complex or an insular attitude, to become a champion. He became one of the most feared swimmers in Britain.

His greatest motivator was Linford Christie – and his breaststroke was nowhere near as good as Darren's. His swimming idols were Duncan Goodhew, Adrian Moorhouse and Nick Gillingham.

By the time he was 15 he'd won two gold medals in the nationals. Suddenly, that early morning slog of pre-school pool training on wet and cold Freshwater mornings had seemed all worthwhile.

When he went to Bath University to join their group of a dozen elite swimmers a successful career looked a certainty – and so it proved. I could fill this chapter by just naming his swimming achievements against world class opposition. He took on champions and beat them.

Darren has always paid tribute to his parents, Alan and Barbara, for all of their continual support. They were so thrilled when, as a lanky eight-year old, he won the West Wight club's under-nines breaststroke title. That certainly was the start of something big.

I love the story of a Darren Mew record that might never be beaten. It's London to Portsmouth, by train. It took him six hours. He went via Eastbourne, after boarding the wrong train!

For ten years he was ranked in the world's top ten breaststroke swimmers. What a story for a kid from Totland Bay!

CHAPTER 15

Derek Hunt

THE FIRST TIME I ever saw Derek Hunt was on the back of his fruit and vegetable lorry selling as if there was a famine imminent. He probably told his customers there was! It was the perfect job for a likeable man who has the gift of the gab – and more. I love self-made people and Derek was certainly that. He took on the Island's big boys and became our most successful wholesaler.

Derek, never afraid to speak his mind, readily admitted he was inspired by one of his chief rivals. During one of our several interviews he told me: "The late Ron Ash, who worked for Pattie's, was my great hero. He could sell snow to Eskimos. When you started up a new round, if you beat him to the call on the first Monday morning in his Cowes territory, you were certainly second the next morning."

In 1964, around the early days of his own business, Derek would catch the 6am ferry to Southampton to buy his produce, arrive back at Rookley at 10-30am, load the lorry and go out on the round. He was back for a meal at 4-30pm and then, in summer, would work in his growing field until 9pm.

Hundreds of Islanders will remember those wild country music Saturday nights at his Pagham Place warehouse. They were 12 memorable years – and no posh seats. Most people sat on straw bales. Today's health and safety brigade would have had a field day. Derek was licensed for 240 punters but for top acts like The Cotton Mill Boys and Shag Connors and the Carrot Crunchers, add a 100 or two more. I loved getting interviews less than two miles from home. There were some great artists, including Leapy Lee and George Moody plus genuine American acts like Rattlesnake Annie, Jimmy Lawton, JR Williams and Wesley Parker. There was no rip-off. The tickets were just £2-50.

"We cleared the fruit and veg out on Saturday mornings, swept it clean, then brought in the straw bales, tables and chairs and the bar. They loved sitting on the bales and the acoustics were brilliant. Martin Chambers, a local country music nut, gave me so much help."

There was a particularly sad moment when the legendary Shag Connors came for, what proved to be, his final concert. He was taken ill just a couple of days later and passed away. When he sang his own song, The Cotswolds, you could hear a pin drop. They always had a live cockerel on stage, which delighted the fans.

In the early days, many of his stars stayed the night at the hotel just a few doors up. Well, actually, it was Derek's house and he and Gail vacated their bedroom to sleep on the floor.

What an all-rounder! Derek was the Island's old banger racing champion for three consecutive years. He's also got more buses than they had on TV's *On The Buses*. He's restored double deckers, one of which ended up in Japan. His Seaview Services double decker was seen on television's *Alfresco*, with him driving.

Derek still loves his country music and his show on Angel Radio is, amazingly, listened to by fans in America. How's that for a turnaround!

CHAPTER 16

Michael Sheard

TALKING TO Michael Sheard was such an enjoyable experience – and you didn't have to do much. He could relate stories about working with some of the greatest stars in the world, being the scary Mr Bronson to millions of *Grange Hill* fans and, of course, enthuse about his love for the Island.

The son of an Aberdeen minister, he had an early dream of becoming a farmer but after his debut in an amateur stage play, as a 12-year old, his ambition changed for ever.

He studied at RADA and, ironically, his first pro job was back home in a Perth repertory company. That led to a marvellous career on stage and screen.

Michael rang me on one occasion to see if I had a black Crombie overcoat. Merely working for a local radio station, I was not in the habit of wearing a £600 coat. I did have a modest Burton's black imitation. It looked good on television when Michael borrowed it to read a Tennyson poem on Freshwater Downs. When he brought it back my son, Sean, answered the door and froze for a minute, as Mr Bronson handed him dad's coat.

I know during the repeats of Grange Hill a young lad ran out of a Ryde school and straight into Michael. He looked terrified and pleaded " I'm so sorry sir." I'm sure he expected the cry of "you, boy!" from Mr Bronson.

Michael's television appearances were so varied. There was Herr Grunwold in *Auf Weidersehen Pet*, Arthur Dabner, Emily Bishop's boyfriend, in *Corrie* and guest appearances in *The Likely Lads*, *On The Buses*, *Dixon Of Dock Green* and numerous *Dr Who*'s.

On the big screen he played Hitler in *Indiana Jones And The Last Crusade*, Admiral Ozzel in *The Empire Strikes Back* and was seen in *The Riddle Of The Sands*, *The Dirty Dozen* and *High Road to China*, plus many others. Sometimes, he died in the first ten minutes.

This precise wording would have produced one of his beaming smiles. Those who worked with Michael Sheard included Sean Connery, Harrison Ford, Roger Moore, who wrote the foreword to his first book, David Niven, John Wayne and Laurence Olivier.

The stars loved Michael because he had a fund of stories and was larger than life. He was also much happier being a support actor.

The first time we met, in 1989, he told me: "I don't want to be a star. I'd simply hate it. I can still go into a shop and buy a loaf of bread and not be mobbed."

I think when Michael started doing conventions he realised he was more famous than he imagined. At *Star Wars* and *Dr Who* events hundreds wanted to talk to him. Michael sometimes did several in the same weekend. He was also very shrewd and began writing a series of memoirs, which were eagerly bought at conventions.

Michael and his family first came to the Island for camping holidays and those happy times encouraged them to move here in the 1980s. In his home town of Ryde he was a regular sight in faded old shorts and t-shirt. He loved the friendship of locals and was always ready to help charity functions.

Sadly, Michael died in 2005 at the age of just 65. He was an inspirational man and had the priceless gift of making people happy. I once went to a dinner party at the home of highly acclaimed cinematographer Gilbert Taylor. Who was the life and soul of the night? You know the answer, anyway.

The day Michael died the family posted his pre-planned farewell curtain speech online. It simply said: "Thank you my Very Dear Chums – See ya." I was just proud to have known him.

CHAPTER 17

Brian Greening & Bill Shepard

WHEN I USED to watch a spotty faced Brian Greening play for East Cowes Vics, I never imagined he would go on to become the Island's most prolific author. During his football life he'd been a prolific goalscorer but later used much more energy writing books than he ever did on a soccer field.

Keith Newbery named him 'Grumpy' Greening. None of us who knew him would disagree with that – but we love him for it. He was always my radio standby, in case I had a space to fill. On one occasion, he had Bill Shepard with him. Bill said a few words towards the end but he was back in his own right very soon afterwards. Since then, Greening and Shepard have become the Island's favourite double act. They even played to a full house at the Quay Arts Centre.

Bill has a story for every occasion. When we met for 'Grumpy's' 2017 Christmas lunch at Newport Golf Club, Bill reminded me that he had worked at the Wootton Crematorium for 22 years and during that period he undertook the first 10,000 cremations. Not an obvious conversation for a Sunday lunch.

Mr Greening, probably not the Island's answer to Shakespeare, has put many of Bill's great stories into print.

On our first major interview, Bill had a few surprises in store. His family never had a bible in the house and he was never christened. There was more to come. He'd never seen a football or cricket match, had no television, computer or mobile phone and only listened to the radio twice a day, for the weather and news.

The Shepard family had little money and his father earned about £2 a week. Any more, was made by bartering.

When Bill was just two, he wandered off from his home, next to where the bus station is today, and was spotted down at Pan Mill watching the ducks. Cars were a rare sight in those days. No one locked their doors in Bill's street. They used to fatten up two pigs every year and with no back entrance they had to walk them in and out through the house.

Bill Shepard, left, and Brian Greening

"We used to walk them out of the front door and back again. Then they didn't worry the last time they went out and never came back," reflected Bill.

How times have changed. When Bill was a young schoolboy he would go down to Newport Quay and hitch a day's outing with lorry drivers. He still fondly remembered having a special day out on a steam wagon. Later on in life, he was never afraid of hard work and sometimes had several jobs going. Often he would work into the early hours. A good recipe for living into his 90s.

Both Bill and Brian are Barton Boneheads – and proud of it.

I've written much about Brian Greening in past years and he's never told me if he liked it or not. He's never sued, anyway.

He did leave East Cowes Vics to become a professional footballer. He moved to Sandown FC and was paid £2-50 a week. At that time, he was only earning £10 a week in his full-time job. He also played in what has been described as the finest match ever seen on the Island. It was at Seaclose and Seaview beat Parkhurst 7-6. I wore a brand new overcoat to the match and tore it on barbed wire.

When you phone Brian up, the calls are screened and a voice asks you who you are. That's the price of fame!!

CHAPTER 18

Pamela Green

IN 1993 I invited Yarmouth's Douglas Webb to appear live on my radio show. He had a great story, having been a top London photographer and a real life Dam Buster. His still photos were used in the opening credits of the hit TV series *The Sweeney*. He brought his wife Pam in with him and revealed, which probably is the right word, that she was Pamela Green, the most famous British nude model of the '50s and '60s. Not surprisingly, she came back twice more to talk about her own life.

We became friends and I asked Pam if she would let my daughter come out to see some of her period costumes, to help with her studies at an art college in Bournemouth. I'll never forget that night. Pam wore the costumes on top of her own clothes and then suddenly got frustrated. With that, she stripped down to her bra and pants, to make it easier. The curtains were open and the light was on but I guess residents of Ommaney Road were used to that.

Pam had first taken her clothes off in the late '40s, mainly for art schools and local amateur photographers. It was five shillings an hour if you appeared nude but only 4/6d if you kept them on.

She was told professional photographers paid more and one day she took a walk down London's Greek Street and went into Douglas Webb's famous studio.

"I asked him if he needed nude models and he told me to take my clothes off. He looked at my figure and said 'you'll do' and booked me for a session.

"At the end of my first shoot he asked me to sign a release form. When I put on my school scarf he suddenly discovered that I was a 17 year old schoolgirl. He was rather shocked. As I was under 21, my parents had to sign the form. They didn't mind at all," said Pam.

In the '50s, her fame spread and she appeared alongside Audrey Hepburn in Cidal Soap adverts. Douglas, who became her husband, marketed sets of five nude pictures of Pam for the ready made London market, particularly on Cup Final days.

Naked As Nature Intended was her first movie and others included *Peeping Tom*, in which she was the first person to appear completely nude in a British feature film. A few years later when a clip of another, called *The Window Dresser*, was seen on television, with Pam only wearing a hat, it upset a lady so much she wrote to *Women's Hour*.

"She said it was disgusting and her children were ruined for life – but she didn't mention her husband. We were invited on to *Women's Hour* to fight it out but she didn't turn up.

"I was interviewed on my own and at the end I said that in the Bible it says they were naked and not ashamed. If it was good enough for God, it was good enough for me. They used a clip of this many times."

Pam caused a stir when she first joined the Yarmouth WI. It was rumoured at the time that some of the husbands had been fans of Pam, during her more exposed days.

When Douglas died, Pam became quite lonely and I would see her sat on a seat in Yarmouth Harbour. I would sometimes join her for a chat.

After Pam's death, in 2010, the local WI honoured one of her last requests. She had wanted more people to see her movies – and they did just that at a charity night.

CHAPTER 19

Toni Malo

IN 1976 I was sent a vinyl single by a local folk singer called Toni Malo. On one side was *Ferry To The Isle Of Wight* and the flipside was *Cowes Week*. John Waterman of Solent Records had commissioned him to write two Island comedy songs. At that stage, I didn't know his past life had included being a tattooist, croupier, commercial artist and the owner of a nude studio. From the inside, at Her Majesty's pleasure, he'd also found out crime doesn't pay. Life got better and he met movie legends that included Jayne Mansfield, Marilyn Monroe and Herbert Lom.

Toni, who ran Curios in Cowes and later a western shop in Union Street, Ryde, was great company and he had a story for every occasion. He had a black belt in Taekwondo, was a very inspirational local snooker coach and such a good songwriter.

His musical career had begun in Oxford. Both he and Pam Ayres started together at the city's BBC local radio station. During his career he supported the Rolling Stones and Pink Floyd, at rag balls, and sang on Radio 1. In nearby Headington he also had his nude studio.

"We had students come in from the university looking to earn some money. There were a lot of funny looking men wearing glasses and carrying plastic macs and cameras. I was never sure they even had film in their cameras," said Toni.

In more recent years he could have made a fortune as a tattooist. Once he had a dissatisfied customer who came back because it had fallen off.

No one ever tired of Toni's story about Marilyn Monroe – except him. He'd told it so many times. He was only the second person I had ever met who had been kissed by Marilyn. The first was Frankie Vaughan. They had made an American movie together. In fact, Toni worked as a drape at Pinewood Studios for a while, which is where he met Miss Monroe. They did have a few quick conversations in between takes of the movie called *The Prince And The Showgirl*. He really took to her.

"I had to stand hidden from view at the top of the stairs to pull a piece of cotton along. On screen, it gave the effect the wind was blowing. She did about 76 takes and on a really good one she saw me and said 'so that's how you do it'. So that was ruined and we had to do a few more.

"She never washed very much and it was make-up on top of make-up. One day I heard Laurence Olivier, who was also starring in the movie, say to her 'oh dear Marilyn, you do smell.' I hope that doesn't upset anyone," said Toni.

I first saw him sing at the popular folk nights at the Sloop, Wootton. He had quite a following there and they certainly went out and bought his single. It seemed, throughout his life, Toni was discovered about every five years. He had dreamed of becoming a cult figure – and he certainly achieved that on the Isle of Wight. During his long career he was pressurised by people in the business which put him off completely.

Once he rang me up to ask if I knew anyone who could play a little bit of keyboard for a demo tape he was making. My son, Sean, quickly volunteered and was heard on the track. Toni, himself, was a very talented musician and could play mouth harp and six-string, twelve-string and slide guitars.

CHAPTER 20

Laura Michelle Kelly

WHEN I FIRST SAW Laura Michelle Kelly she was playing bit parts and in the chorus of local shows at Sandown Pavilion and Shanklin Theatre. I never expected to go to London a few years later to meet her at the Aldwych Theatre and, en route, see her face all over the underground posters and looking down at me from a red double decker bus. That was the day I knew she'd made the big time.

I could barely control my emotions when she first came on stage in *Whistle Down The Wind*. Being an Islander, it meant something rather special.

Laura had no formal training and did not go to a drama school or academy. That made her a role model for so many Island youngsters. It was hard work, though. She queued around a theatre to get an audition for *Beauty And The Beast*. Several months later she was playing the lead at some performances. In the wake of that hit show came others like *Fiddler On The Roof*, *My Fair Lady*, *Les Miserables*, *Mamma Mia* and *Mary Poppins*. It has continued with starring roles on Broadway in *Mary Poppins*, *Fiddler On The Roof*, *Finding Neverland* and *The King And* I.

The Kelly family, all such nice people, have firm Christian beliefs and Laura prays before every performance. I loved their company and it was sad when they moved to America.

I'll never forget how kind Laura and her father, Martin, were in 2006, when my wife was seriously ill in St Mary's Hospital. They came into the radio station and the three of us shared a very emotional hug and a prayer. Martin actually made a point of going to see my wife and she was so touched by this. Sadly, she didn't make it.

Laura never forgot her Island roots and often when local coach parties went up to London to see her shows, she went on board, just before they left, to thank them for coming.

One of my favourite pictures of her is painting the front door of their Sandown home, wearing a boiler suit. I have never released this to be seen in public. It might have made *The Sun*, too.

There have been so many highlights during her fantastic career and I remember the night I tempted her back to Shanklin to present some trophies at the Island Amateur Theatre Awards. There was a huge reception when she came on, as a surprise guest.

Who would have thought she would make the movie *The Goddess*, with Ronan Keating? He had this to say about her. "Laura Michelle Kelly is one of the best singers I have ever worked with. She has a brilliant and stunning voice."

Many discovered that fact when she released her amazing debut pop album, *The Storm Inside*. She co-wrote some of the superb songs.

Laura won an Olivier Award for *Mary Poppins*, was in the hit movie *Sweeney Todd* and was so thrilled to receive a good luck message from Dame Judi Dench on the opening night of *My Fair Lady*. The Queen also came to see her in this production. It was a private visit but she did meet Her Majesty.

Whenever I have met Laura she has always been keen to pay tribute to her former Island singing teacher Barbara Walter. Sadly, the lovely Welsh lady is no longer with us. They were great for each other.

Laura has come a long way since her Shanklin Theatre debut in David Redston and Tony Wright's fantastic musical A *Christmas Carol*. She was also in another of their triumphs, *Notre Dame*.

CHAPTER 21

Alan Titchmarsh

MY INTRODUCTION to Alan Titchmarsh came from a mutual friend, the wonderful actor Reginald Marsh, famous for hit series that included *Terry And June*, *Coronation Street*, *The Good Life* and *George And Mildred*. Reg did such a lot for MENCAP and, in particular, their local project at Ryde's Haylands Farm. Alan came to the centre several times and was such a welcome visitor. The students loved him.

I've known Alan nearly 30 years and have been thrilled by his media success that has made him one of the most famous people in Britain. I have heard of some presenters who were jealous of his burgeoning broadcasting career, after, initially, being known purely as a gardener. Alan is a man who is prepared to accept a challenge and he has the skills to make a real success of so many things. His daytime television chat shows had a huge following and his *Ground Force* was enjoyed by millions of fans. I can remember going to London to interview him to promote one of his novels. I had read it and was able to tease him about one or two steamy passages, which he just laughed off. His hit books endeared him even more to the ladies who swooned over his television appearances.

Amateur dramatics inspired Alan to aim for a career in television. Prior to his media fame, he worked at Kew Gardens, as a gardener and teacher. One evening I was at the Trinity Theatre, Cowes, to review a play and Alan and his wife, Alison, walked in. He had a keen interest in the Cowes AODS. Many years later he actually appeared as the narrator in a top West End production of *Wind In The Willows*.

Daytime Live, from Pebble Mill, was another Titchmarsh gem. He told me, back in 1989: "I try and approach every programme as if it's going to be the best *Daytime Live* ever. That's the only way I can work. Sometimes you can be disappointed but I think the programme standard is high."

Alan has always been a workaholic – and there's nothing wrong with that. The last time I interviewed him, at his new Cowes home, he had popped down to make an appearance at the IW College. True to form, he promised to see me for around 30 minutes, just before he headed to Newport. I left him just about to tuck into a plate of sausages. He had not long moved into the house and I deliberately didn't look at his garden. I think it was work in progress – and I didn't trip over any decking!

When he became the Island's High Sheriff, I was flattered to be one of just two local journalists invited to the Holmwood Hotel, Cowes, to interview him. The other being the very talented and rather witty ex-*County Press* reporter Richard Wright.

Alan deserved that honour and he did so much to put the Island on the map. He even managed to clear a whole year to carry out his duties and proved to be one of the very best we have ever had.

I have only ever met two famous people with amazing photographic memories. The first was Bob Monkhouse, who never forgot a name, and the second is Alan Titchmarsh. Obviously, we had known each other for a long time but a few years ago he met my partner, Bertie, for the first time. There was a gap of several years before he met her again – and he'd remembered her name. Quite remarkable.

Talking of names, he has forgiven me for the very first time we met, back in the '80s. I recorded the interview and mispronounced his name and introduced him as Titmarsh. He loved it.

CHAPTER 22

Carl Prean

I LOVE THE legendary story of a local village table tennis player who gave up the game minutes after he'd been beaten by a seven year old boy, who, it seemed, could barely see over the table. A few years later that defeat must have been much easier to accept. That same young boy, Carl Prean, was Britain's number one, rated ninth in Europe and was in the world's top 20 players.

I've met up with him several times and he was always pleased when I invited him on to my radio show, as I let him choose his favourite soul records. Somehow, I don't

think Carl has ever got the local acclaim he deserves. If he'd been Britain's top footballer or cricketer, it would have been a different story. To some, table tennis is not a glamorous sport but Carl's fame, within the sport, spread all over the world, from Russia to the Far East.

There were sometimes Island rumours that Carl's parents, John and Erica, had virtually pushed him into the game but this was way off course.

"I loved table tennis and started playing when I was six. We had a table at home and at Columbia Products, my dad's factory, where there were great facilities. In the summer talented players would come over from the mainland to practice with me and improve my game. I probably played three or four times a week," said Carl.

I loved his incentive to have a personal goal throughout his career. In the very early days it was simply to beat the Island's best player, the very talented Jim Daly. Carl will never forget that night. Years later, Carl achieved another fantastic milestone. He actually beat the current world champion of the time, Jorgen Persson.

During an eight year spell Carl represented England on many occasions. Once when England beat Russia 5-4, he won three games to earn the victory. In 1983 he helped England take a surprise bronze medal in the Tokyo World Championships. He won the England singles title on several occasions and made the last 16 in the 1992 Barcelona Olympics. His other memories include winning the Belgium Open and getting to the final of the USA Open.

In 1990 two million television viewers tuned in to see Carl beat his arch English rival Desmond Douglas, to win the *Daily Telegraph* Masters.

Carl played in the famous German Bundesliga for many years and for key games there were often crowds of around 3000. The teams were run like football clubs. He also played in the French League.

When I last interviewed Carl, he had retired from the game and he told me why. "I finally retired because I'd had enough of the game and had played for well over 30 years. I exceeded all my expectations and travelled all over the world. Now I just do a little coaching."

He loves cricket and particularly Hampshire. We both know they are such a frustrating team to support. He has played himself for Ryde, Shanklin and Brading.

Carl was so thrilled when they named the Smallbrook Table Tennis Centre after him. It was an honour so richly deserved. He won the Island singles title at the age of 11 – and just never looked back.

Ray Rowsell

RAY ROWSELL moved to the Island in 1952 to become a Newport policeman, which eventually led him to become the very popular Bembridge bobby. He soon settled into local life and appeared in productions for the Newport Amateur Dramatic Society, produced hit musicals at Sandown Pavilion, was known for his yodelling skills and helped form the IW Youth Concert Band. His greatest moment must have been racing along Bembridge beach in the dramatic final scene of the movie *Something To Hide*, which starred Peter Finch.

His last ever job was being the night manager at Warner's, Bembridge Coast. I met him so many times when I was there to interview visiting cabaret stars. Somehow, he always produced a cup of tea. I was also rather lucky. I managed to miss most of his yodelling sessions! We all teased him about those.

Ray had travelled all over the world in the military police, during his national service days, and after his demob he joined the Air Ministry Constabulary at Boscombe Down and later worked in Cyprus.

When he first arrived in Bembridge he was asked if he would like to form a new youth club. Vandalism had closed the only previous one.

Ray told me: "I had no money to really get it going, so we organised a series of donkey derbies to boost the funds. We were lucky to get some big names to make appearances.

"Over the years we had Norman Wisdom, Ray Alan and Lord Charles, Mollie Sugden, the whole of the *Dad's Army* team, Linda Hayden, another star from *Something To Hide*, and both Cliff Michelmore and Jean Metcalfe."

They did their own youth club shows and the girls were more up for it than the boys. Ray had the perfect solution,

"The only way I could get the boys in was to present minstrel shows and black them up. They didn't mind because the audiences didn't know who they were." That couldn't happen anymore.

In all, Ray produced six shows and local personalities like Sybil Johns, Tony Brett, Charlie Martin, Reg and Kay Milton and Noel Watkin willingly took part.

I never tired of his *Something To Hide* memories and he was never allowed to forget it. He had to get special permission from the police authorities to appear in it.

"Peter Finch was seen to shoot John Stride, the police sergeant in the film, and with that I drove up with several local policeman and chased Peter along the beach. Just as we got to him, he shot himself and fell on a sand castle.

"The only problem was the hanging about. We must have had at least half a dozen takes."

In the movie Ray is the leading policeman in the final chase – and he didn't even get time to yodel.

When the film was shown at the Savoy Cinema, Newport, the whole audience cheered when Ray and his police colleagues raced across the screen in pursuit of Peter Finch. They issued a CD of the music, written by Roy Budd, and guess who could be seen on the cover?

Ray Rowsell, a gifted and unassuming community worker, helped to form the Bembridge Youth Club Band, which later became the IW Youth Concert Band.

They appeared all over the world, made albums and were seen on TV's *Songs Of Praise*. Ray, as ever, was always keen to praise others and told me during one of our interviews: "It was all down to Maurice Keat that we suddenly had great success."

What luck it was that Ray got stationed here back in 1952. An unforgettable character.

CHAPTER 24

Jeff Hose

WHEN JEFF HOSE was the most hostile fast bowler on the Island he would hurtle down the hill at Ventnor's Steephill ground and was a fearsome sight as he fired cricket balls all around you. He was supremely confident and looked exceptionally tall as he raced in to bowl just 22 yards away from you. He seemed invincible – or did he?

When not facing him, he was a hero to many of us. Off the field, you just couldn't meet a nicer guy. In the early '90s, I stopped him in his tracks. I had hit him for a six on one memorable day but it wasn't that. I invited him to appear live on to my IW Radio chat show and he suddenly froze – like a lot of batsmen who faced him. I couldn't believe it.

"Sorry John, I just couldn't do anything like that. It's too frightening," said one of our local sporting icons. I even promised to pre-record it at his home but even that fell on deaf ears. I tried to bribe him by offering to plug Hose, Rhodes and Dickson and that was turned down. Luckily, I have written a few newspaper and magazine articles on him in past years.

The last time I interviewed him was in the Ventnor office of Hose, Rhodes and Dickson. There he was with that beaming smile – and the very fashionable stubble. As soon as we'd finished, he was off to sell a house in Niton. Actually, I think my sister, Celia, kept him in business for a while!

Jeff was a brilliant cricket all-rounder. He once took all 10 wickets for just 25 runs, on another occasion he smashed an unbeaten 152 and to complete a memorable hat trick once hit six 6's in an over. He was our own Gary Sobers.

He once told me: "When I first came to the Island it was a choice of either Ventnor or their old enemy Shanklin. Over the years a lot of Ventnor players have told me I should have joined Shanklin – but that's another story."

Jeff was unlucky to be spotted just too late in his sporting life. County clubs are always looking for young players. He did have trials with Hampshire 2nd XI but was well into

his 20s. He was once told by an ex-county cricketer that he could have made it. Jeff was the first Island cricketer to enjoy success in the highly rated Southern Cricket League. He joined Lymington and helped them win the title. They fielded some top class cricketers, including several who had played county cricket.

Luckily, any regrets Jeff might have had were suddenly blown away when his son, Adam, broke into county cricket with Somerset, following his spell as a professional cricketer with the MCC. Then he was headhunted by Warwickshire and was seen batting like dad, in front of the TV cameras. Ironically, he had trials with Hampshire but was never taken on the staff. Too often, they seem to prefer to import has-beens, who continually break down.

Jeff, who has spent well over 40 years on the Island, came here via Liverpool, Northern Ireland and India. He became a trainee estate agent at Sir Francis Pittis and then joined Players as a cigarette salesman. Later he returned to Pittis to manage their Newport office before forming Hose, Rhodes and Dickson, with his wife Jill and Mark Rhodes. From humble beginnings they have gone on to employ 50 staff.

He also played local rugby, football and badminton but is most famous for cricket and selling houses.

CHAPTER 25

Wally Edwards

KNOWING WALLY EDWARDS was one of the delights of Island life. Over the years thousands of customers enjoyed the banter during his 39 years on Southern Vectis buses. He was unique. The only one ever to give green shield stamps and free suntan oil. He'd also go off route to drop someone home. In the course of his job, he rushed into a burning house to rescue two boys and then went back for the mother, who was asleep. Lord Louis Mountbatten later gave him a special award for this.

A lady from Seaview once summed up Wally perfectly. She told him: "What we have gained on the Island from you is what Jamaica has lost." He just loved people – and we all loved him.

He even met his lovely wife Shirley on his bus and he told me once: "I fell in love with her the very first time I saw her."

In 2013, the last time I interviewed him, he told me about the great gift of his family. "Our family have been so good to us and to think I was a bit frightened when I asked Shirley's mum if I could marry her."

In the early days of his job with Southern Vectis, his workmates had plenty of names for him. He accepted them all with his usual good grace and willingly joined in their fun. Now the PC brigade would not permit it. On one

Wally and Shirley Edwards

occasion he continued to work during industrial action and was called a blackleg by a colleague. His instant reply was "yes, I've got two."

Once, a few minutes after Wally had left a Ryde bus stop, a lady screamed out that she'd left her baby behind. He doubled back and the baby was still sitting happily in the pram.

Early one dark winter morning, at just after 6am, Wally was driving his bus from Haylands to Havenstreet when he passed two young children with a torch. They were walking to Binstead to see a baby. Wally picked them up and eventually saw a postman in Havenstreet who took them back to the farmhouse where they lived. Their mother, who knew nothing about their adventure until they mentioned the bus ride, went to Wally's home in the evening to thank him.

It happened again in Wootton when he found two young children walking from East Cowes to Ryde, at 6-30 in the morning. The boy was intent on seeing his real dad in Ryde. Wally took them back to their home in East Cowes.

Wally's four-hour Round the Island trip meant Southern Vectis were flooded with letters of appreciation from visitors.

"It was a business. I used to stand in the bus station and sell them the trip that cost less than £5. If I got people on the buses the company could still employ me. I often got a round of applause at the end of the trip, which was a real bonus."

Wally was a local magistrate for 17 years and his policy was to do what had to be done but in a fair way. That proved another hugely rewarding part of his life. Raising money for the EM Hospice also brought him great satisfaction. Sadly, he needed it himself during the latter stages of his life.

In 1996 he went to Buckingham Palace to receive his MBE from the Queen and it was so well deserved.

"I was told the Queen would not say very much. For some reason she talked to me for quite a while, particularly when she found out I came from the Island." I hope he didn't offer her green shield stamps or suntan lotion!

CHAPTER 26

Stephen Wight

WHEN I HAD a phone call from Zoe Young, from East Cowes, to say that her daughter, Claire, had recently seen one of her school pals, called Stephen Gray, in an episode of *A Touch Of Frost*, I became quite excited. It got even better because he'd gone to my old school, Grange Road Primary. There had been a name change – of course. It seemed rather appropriate, too. He was now called Stephen Wight.

After quickly making contact, we met up in London on several occasions. With his in-

laws living in the West Wight, we also got together a couple of times on home territory. Stephen is such a credit to the Island and the acting profession. He always goes out of his way to meet fans and has also told me, on several occasions, that he will always find the time for us to meet up for another interview.

During his career he's been seen playing major roles in *Diamond Geezer*, with David Jason, *Fingersmith*, *The Paradise*, *New Tricks*, *Sherlock*, *Ashes To Ashes*, *Bluestone 42*, *Whites* and *Threesome*. His movies include *Wilderness*, *Highlander - The Source* and *Weekender*. He was also in the Olivier Award-winning West End production of *The Ladykillers*.

I interviewed him for over 30 minutes at the Gielgud Theatre, after a matinee of *The Ladykillers*, and fans were still waiting outside to see him.

When I saw him play McQueen, the late fashion designer, at the St James Theatre, London, he was sensational. I loved the way he was on stage several minutes before the show actually started. It was so effective and I found his whole performance so emotional. He'd actually shaved his head and grown facial hair to play the part but was still recognised in the street because of the posters on tube stations and buses. In between shows he donned his baseball cap and kept his head down as he went for a break. The way he played McQueen, he certainly needed to get right away for an hour or so.

I never tire of the story of how young Islander Stephen Gray got into acting. After Grange Road, he went to Osborne Middle and then Medina High. Our story begins at the latter.

He was one of three boys who blagged their way into an early lunch. Hunger had set in and they knew they could get away with it, as potential young actors were allowed to go in first, if they were going to attend an audition. Their plan was to play football, instead. They didn't get away with it. Drama teacher Miss Peck rumbled their ruse and, as a punishment, made them audition. How lucky he was. He passed the audition and has never stopped acting since.

Lisa Peck once told me: "Stephen had such a presence on stage, from the very first time I saw him. He was a very brave young actor. When he played Fyedka in our school production of *Fiddler On The Roof*, he had to undertake his first stage kiss. I had to tell him to stop messing about and get on with it."

I did hear rumours that it was the first time he'd ever kissed a girl. I never believed it.

Thankfully, the Island has always had some excellent local amateur theatre companies and he joined one of the best, of that period, The Ferret Theatre Company, run by Graham McFarland. They inspired him even more.

I also witnessed a Wight double in the McQueen show. My daughter, Caroline, was the head of wardrobe. They often reminisced about their old teachers at Medina High. I bet Miss Peck got a mention.

CHAPTER 27

Peter & Margaret Butler

I'VE ALWAYS HAD great admiration for East Cowes couple Peter and Margaret Butler. Peter was one of my first local sporting heroes, particularly when he played for Pompey Juniors, and Margaret Dennis, as she was, was in the same class as me at school. They have been married over 50 years and enjoyed successful sporting careers.

When Margaret first noticed Peter, at Cowes Secondary Modern, he was sat on a radiator. She'd just come in from waiting outside in the cold. It was one of his perks of being head boy. She could never have perceived their future together – on and off the golf course.

Peter was such a gifted sportsman. He was a sprinter for Hampshire Schools and a supremely talented cricketer for Northwood CC. His speed as a winger took him to Fratton Park and we all held our breath. Just a few years earlier Pompey had been the greatest team in the land – twice.

"I was actually asked if I wanted sign as a full professional with Portsmouth but my father said no and that I needed to get a proper job." reflected Peter.

Dad was probably right. Footballers were poorly paid in those days and Peter ended up as a financial controller for GKN. He did enjoy local football for Newport, East Cowes Vics , Cowes and Saro Sports.

Margaret had little hope of not playing golf. Her parents both played at Osborne but she was never that keen – until she met her old head boy. Her father had persuaded Peter to play golf at Osborne and, suddenly, she took a lot more interest in the game – or him, to be exact.

"My dad had brought Peter to the golf club and I knew how long it took to play, so I began seeing a bit more of him," said Margaret.

Peter and Margaret have a joint love of sport and on a few occasions formed a golfing double act of mixed pairs. It was not an inspired decision and there was a little fairway trouble on a few occasions.

Margaret once admitted: "Mixed golf is not really good for a marriage and I did have a little bunker trouble on one occasion." I don't think her older partner was too amused.

Despite having their three children, Margaret was always a member of the Osborne club and over the years scooped so many honours. She first won the Island Ladies championship in 1979 and went on to win it at least six more times. She played for Hampshire, a rare honour, captained the Island team and managed our Inter Island Games team. I'm not sure who would have won an M Butler v P Butler golf challenge – but I have a good idea.

Peter has certainly put a lot back into the game he loved. Since giving up football, he has done so much administration work for both the Island and Hampshire Football Associations.

It's been such a personal pleasure to have known them for many years. I still see them occasionally, with their trolley. No, not on the golf course – shopping in Sainsbury's. Margaret's former golfing partner does not always seem happy to be there. At least, there aren't any bunkers!

CHAPTER 28

James Pellow

SOME ISLANDERS have had the confidence to follow their dreams and others have just lacked the courage to cross the Solent and take on the outside world. Back in 2002, James Pellow, a much-celebrated local actor, decided to leave Ryde for the London Centre of Theatre Studies, to train for a new career as a professional actor. He didn't expect to be the new Olivier, Albert Finney or Alan Bates but took the gamble. He's never regretted it.

It was a far cry from working in Pack and Cullifords for 20 years and later managing the Youth Trust charity shop in Newport. As a local lay preacher, with his heavenly voice, dare I say he fluttered the hearts of a few Methodist maiden ladies. They also equally enjoyed him boldly wearing dresses in his numerous dame roles in pantomime.

Thousands of Radio Solent fans had also enjoyed his regular broadcasts on the *Morning Thought* programme. Around the local WI's, he was also a hit with his monologues and humorous recitations.

It was 15 years after being inspired by the Belle Vue Players production of A *Letter From The General*, that he was persuaded to try amateur dramatics.

James recalled that moment: "I was quite surprised when Joan Hutchinson asked me. I had never really thought of acting and had often wondered how they managed to remember all those lines. I asked when the next rehearsal was and was told it was that evening. I went and got the part of a baddie in *Murder In Company*."

Joining the resident Shanklin Theatre company in 1992 was perfectly timed. Suddenly, he was working with seasoned professionals like Jack Douglas and Tony Adams. James also played in several of their Island premieres. He portrayed Mr Feziwig in their brilliant David Redston and Tony Wright musical A *Christmas Carol*. This was a far better musical than the Leslie Bricusse adaptation called *Scrooge*. Many still talk about the time James played the Hunchback in *Notre Dame*. Despite just having only one line in the script, he gave a very mesmerising visual performance throughout the production.

Amazingly, James was 47 when he finally became a professional actor. He was also aware that Dame Edith Evans and Buster Merrifield were both older than him when they took the same journey.

James became a kind of matinee idol in Sidmouth and was an instant hit with the blue rinse brigade. He spent several summers there in repertory. Then he moved into presenting his one-man shows and these proved so successful in Devon and far beyond.

There was great excitement when James played Lady Bracknell in a West End production of T*he Importance Of Being Ernest*, at the Jermyn Street Theatre. He won rave reviews and roars of approval for that special line "a handbag!" He's performed in professional pantomimes and plays all over Britain, including several with famous television faces.

In 2016 James brought his fantastic one-man show, *Lady Bracknell's Legacy*, back home. This was another ambition and those who went to Newport's Apollo Theatre enjoyed his dual roles of Devonia deRudge and Freddie Farnsworth.

Heather and I had seen Roy Barraclough, who began his professional career at the Atherfield Bay Holiday Camp (more of that later), play a similar dual role, in this case, a brother and sister, in A *Different Way Home*, at the Watford Palace. We told James how brilliant it was and he caught up with it at Basingstoke.

James achieved his ambition and his Island fan club still enjoy his occasional visits to Shanklin Theatre to play in their professional pantomimes. I loved his Shanklin role of Mr Tweedy in *Don't Tell The Wife*, the council worker who was mistaken for a male escort.

CHAPTER 29

Canon James Buckett

FOR YEARS I'd had such admiration for Canon James Buckett. Just days after his retirement I invited him on to my radio show. By the time he was live on-air, I'd already had two surprises. We'd met a few days earlier, when I went to his home to plan the programme. His record choices included Frankie Howerd and I was the first to christen his new garden love seat, donated to him and his wife as a retirement present.

James had such a gift and his well chosen words could either create joy or help others who needed comfort. He did admit to me that he always worked better under pressure and did not like planning too far ahead.

The year of 1966 was rather special. England won the World Cup, a Soviet spacecraft landed on Venus and James Buckett came to St Helens, to become the village priest.

When he first arrived in the summer to meet the local parochial church council, it didn't quite go as well as he'd hoped.

"Not knowing the Island very well, I told them I would be on the ferry that came in at 1-30pm. I hadn't realised that the holidaymakers would be queuing up to catch the ferry to Ryde Pier. I kept them waiting three hours. It was a wonder I got the job."

James loved St Helens and the people of the village. At that time, there were so many characters. One of them was 102-year old Mrs Machin. When James went to her home for the first time, he was surprised to see her doing housework, with a feather duster. He was even more surprised when he bent down and touched her lovely dog, sat near the fire. It was a stuffed animal.

His first wedding in the village did not go to plan. He announced the opening hymn and then nothing happened. A few days later he passed the village newsagents and noticed a placard outside the shop. It read: "Organ breaks down at vicar's first wedding ceremony."

In 1972 James was on a six week cruise on the *Carmania*. There were 600 American doctors and their families on board. He was the priest, representing the Missions To Seafarers. On his return, his wife showed him a letter from the bishop, offering him the move to the Newport Minster Church. He was not seeking a move and was very content in St Helens.

"The bishop wanted me to take up the new appointment and told me his objective for me was to build up the civic and community links with the church. I think I managed to do this during my 23 years."

On one unusual day, James met Lord Louis Mountbatten at three different events. At the first he wore his usual cassock, at the next he was in his army uniform and at the third was in his lounge suit. The ever observant Lord Louis picked up on this and told him: "You have as many changes of clothes as I do."

I loved his story of taking a mainland wedding, as a locum. The bride got stuck in traffic and the best man forgot the ring and went back to find it. When the bride and her father finally arrived, he was told they had the ring – but the best man was still away looking for it. When he returned, the wedding was 45 minutes late. In the vestry, after the ceremony, James proudly took out his fountain pen, only to find it had run out of ink. They had to ask if anyone had another fountain pen.

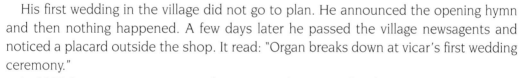

CHAPTER 30

Sy and Isa Lyn

IN 1972 Sy and Isa Lyn came to the Island for a summer season, as a part of the Temperance Seven Show on Shanklin Pier. They liked it so much they didn't go back to the Midlands for very long. They moved to Shanklin and eventually opened their Magic Box, next to Barney's Emporium.

I loved their shop and there was always a hint of mystery when you looked around. They manufactured illusions for magicians all around the world. Their Island exports included head choppers, zig zag ladies and painless surgery. In the early '80s there were only three people in Britain producing large illusion props – and Sy was one of them. The first time I interviewed them they tested out their latest head chopper – and guess whose bonce was placed in the guillotine? I survived to write the article for the *Weekly Post*.

It was a hectic life for them, particularly in summer. Sy made the illusion props by day, Isa looked after the shop and at night they performed their magic act in shows all around the Island. In '76 they were in the summer show at the Ventnor Winter Gardens.

Sy, who had begun his showbiz life as a singer, changed his career by complete accident. He took his eight-year old daughter out to buy her a birthday present and suddenly realised it was half day closing. They found one shop open and there he bought her a David Nixon Magic Box. He practised a few tricks to impress his daughter and loved it so much that he left his singing days behind. Sy's daughter also became rather good and even won the top ladies' award at a Southport magic convention.

Isa also had a showbiz background and they formed a very successful magic act, which brought them to the Island. Their dove magic was quite superb. Top magicians made use of Sy's cabinet making skills and he got to know Tommy Cooper very well. He actually made a harmonium for the comedy legend and Tommy used it on a Royal Variety Show.

Sy and Isa also performed in shows for the Island's Vectis Magicians Club. Their members included John Young, Barry Rutherford and the Amazing Delgados.

They became very excited in early 1982 when I went to tell them that Tommy Cooper had been booked for a short season at Sandown Pavilion. They were clearly hoping he would visit them in their Shanklin shop. They watched him at Sandown Pavilion and a couple of days later he visited them in the Magic Box. I had the tip off and managed to send a photographer to record the memorable moment.

Personally, it was a short Sandown season I will never forget. I went to interview Tommy on opening night and he asked me to come back on other nights just for a post-show friendly chat in his dressing room. What an experience that was.

Sy and Isa with Tommy Cooper

CHAPTER 31

Fred Price

FRED PRICE LIVED in Havenstreet and he was often stood at his front gate to greet whoever walked by. How times had changed in the village. It had become a rat run for commuters. He enjoyed it far more when horse and carts were still in fashion. I first heard him on the Alex Dyke IW Radio phone-in and instantly wanted him on my radio show.

This chat show success led him to become a local personality. He recorded voice-overs for commercials, enjoyed spots on TV and radio and even had a helicopter ride. I'll never forget the day he met the Vernon Girls, when they appeared on the same radio show. Maggie Stredder and the girls had never met anyone quite like him. It was a double mutual admiration society.

In 1993 Fred and I recorded a cassette of his stories and it became the Island's top selling album. That was released to remember two popular Havenstreet characters who had recently died, Fred Winter and John Batten. All the profits went to the Earl Mountbatten Hospice. Later we recorded a video in Fred's garden and that proved very successful.

Fred revealed some great stories from his school days. I loved the one about the day he saw the girl in the next desk copying his work. He revealed it with his delightful rustic accent: "I took hold of her by her gert long plaits and jammed her head in her desk. Didn't she squeal." There were stories of how he got caught out playing truant and how he got away with ringing the school bell at an inappropriate time.

Fred loved the Island and working on local farms. One of his favourite places was Bowcombe Down. He was also a gifted ploughman and sheep shearer.

Meeting a local farmer's daughter changed his life instantly. When Vera Hamer came into his life they became inseparable, until his death in 2012. Although, he did let her go and play bingo every week.

"When Vera and I worked together at Guildford Farm our joint wages were £5.50 a week, with no holidays or overtime. When we got married in 1947 our cottage was worth £200."

There was nothing better than dropping in to see Fred and Vera. They made everybody welcome and her homemade cakes were delicious. He would sit in his favourite chair and put the world to rights but could never come to grips with the changing Island life. On one occasion he told me: "One thing I can't stand is mainland city people moving to the Island and telling us country folk what to do."

Fred had some vivid memories. He joined our wartime committee and worked on farms all over the Island. Most times he had to cycle to places like Hampstead, Niton and Whitwell. Later they supplied motorbikes. He loved Ferguson tractors and had a favourite one until he died. When he first started ploughing, it was behind a horse at a Fishbourne farm.

One day he told me: "I can still vividly remember the date of the first day I went to work at Puck House Farm. It was January 4, 1937, and I was 14. I'd saved up my pennies and could afford a pair of size four boots for work. They were 4/6." In today's money around 22p.

Fred was one of those local characters who could always lift your spirits. When he was the bingo caller at the Towers Holiday Centre, at Thorness, he was an instant hit with the holidaymakers. He gave sheep shearing demonstrations to parties of school children and they loved every minute. Fred came from a unique mould.

CHAPTER 32

Hannah Rochell and Daisy Coulam

BACK IN 2014 I headed for Ryde to catch up with a young lady called Hannah Rochell, to help publicise her new book called E*n Brogue: Love Fashion. Love Shoes. Hate Heels.* I had two surprises. I was wearing my so-called brothel creepers and the first thing she did was to take a picture of them. After our chat, she suggested I might like to interview her very close friend, Daisy Coulam. I did that a couple of weeks later. It only seemed fair that they share this chapter.

Hannah loved growing up on the Island but London was the place to be for a fashion journalist. Initially, she had fancied a career in television and took her degree in theatre and media drama at the University of Glamorgan.

Hannah Rochell

"I actually ended up working at a call centre for Ticketmaster, before moving into the accounts section of Dream Team, the Sky TV football drama. I was even seen as an extra, with a few spoken words, over four seasons," said Hannah.

At the age of 30, she bravely took her career in another direction and went back to college to study fashion journalism. This eventually led to top magazines like E*asy Living* and R*ed.* Her first paid job was in T*he Times* fashion department. This even led to four and a half minute interview with Victoria Beckham.

When we met she was the fashion features editor of I*nStyle* and travelled all over Europe. Her blog on flat shoes became so popular it led to that first book, its subsequent follow-up and an E*vening Standard* column.

Daisy Coulam

Her friend from schooldays, Daisy Coulam, is now a famous television writer. She dreamed about becoming an actor but quickly realised she was not going to rival Sheridan Smith and her ilk. Her idol had always been Anthony Minghella. Daisy was prepared to make the tea in a television office and work her way up. Early jobs were on T*he Bill* and W*here The Heart Is,* which gave her aspirations of becoming a writer. Then it happened. She wrote an episode of D*octors* and then came C*asualty* and H*olby City.*

EastEnders was her major breakthrough and she wrote 26 episodes, over a few years. One episode takes up to two months of continual work.

"I was lucky to work on shows I watched. I'd been an E*astEnders* fan for many years and it was sort of in my blood."

Grantchester gave her career another giant leap and her adaptations, from the original stories by James Runcie, just seemed to get better and better. Their success led to more series of the show and working very closely with hunks like James Norton and Robson Green was an added attraction. Her scripts were superbly crafted and she noticeably became quite a lot bolder in her interpretations. It's become a show not to be missed.

Ryde High School often had a bad press but these two girls have done them proud – and they haven't finished yet.

By the way, Hannah's dad is also featured in this book. He's been such an inspiration to many local musicians. That's Brian Sharpe of Cherokees fame – and others since then.

CHAPTER 33

Lee Bradbury

THE FIRST TIME I ever interviewed Lee Bradbury was in his BMW on the M27. A few years earlier I'd seen him arrive at Smallbrook Stadium, via lorry, helicopter, coach, train and boat, from army duty in Northern Ireland, to play for Cowes against old rivals Newport in the IW Senior Cup semi-final. His two goals helped them win.

Back to the M27. Since that Smallbrook double, Lee had played for Portsmouth, Exeter, Manchester City, Crystal Palace and Birmingham. He was then back at Fratton Park. The various clubs had paid £5.3 million for his services. Amazingly, local manager Dolly Crane had the edge over Frank Clarke, Terry Fenwick and Alan Ball. He'd signed him for nothing. Mind you, it was for Plessey Reserves.

I was told on good authority that Lee, who was born in Cowes, was, initially, a Saints supporter. He did have trials there as a 13-year old but a knee injury ruined his chances. Ironically, a few years later Southampton bid a million or two for him.

My wife and I were once guests at Fratton Park and we sat in the directors box. I had not revealed that we favoured the Saints. As Sandra Smith, who I knew from the Kings Theatre, Southsea, showed us into our seats she whispered "I hope you 'scummers' enjoy the match." We did – and I leapt up three times with great excitement, because Lee scored a hat-trick.

During his first spell at Pompey they sold him for £3.5 million to Manchester City. In a pre-season friendly he scored twice and Eddie Large and the Gallagher brothers must have been over the moon. It took him seven games to score in a league match. The Maine Road fans went wild with excitement. He hadn't got that sort of adulation when he'd scored seven for Plessey – all in the same match.

It did not turn out to be the dream move he had hoped for. Did the price tag affect him?

"I didn't really worry about it. I didn't ask them to pay that sort of money for me. Unfortunately, it didn't happen for me or the team. Being out injured for nearly five months didn't help," reflected Lee.

At times the fans became hostile, which did not help his confidence. In one memorable spell, he scored five goals in ten games. Eventually, he moved to Crystal Palace for £1.5 million. At that time, Manchester City needed the money. How times have changed. They'd now pay £3million for a ball boy! Following his later return to Fratton Park, for whom he made 150 appearances in his two spells, he ended his playing career with stints at Walsall, Oxford, Southend and Bournemouth.

Lee did the Island proud. He played 512 games in the Football League and scored 92 goals. At Bournemouth they also played him in defence and he did a good job. He also had his first taste of management at Dean Court, with a spell of 14 months.

After a spell as a youth coach, back at Portsmouth, he became the manager of Havant and Waterlooville in 2012.

I've always found Lee Bradbury such a likeable and genuine man and he commands great respect from his players.

In 2017 I went to Westleigh Park to see a vital Isthmian League championship decider between Havant and local rivals Bognor. It started late because nearly 5000 turned up. Lee had found out I was in the crowd and made a point of coming over to welcome me. I was so impressed with this gesture. That's a real Islander for you. They won the match and, subsequently, the league title. In 2018 they again won promotiom. This time to the National League.

CHAPTER 34

Peter Bingham

I HAVE ALWAYS loved doing talks for so many different organisations and if I come back with a potential future radio guest or a suggestion for a feature article, I am well content. When I spoke to a very appreciative audience at the Island Sailing Club my hosts were Peter Bingham and his lovely wife Rosemary. Over our dinner conversation I realised a fascinating story was unfolding and Peter was instantly booked for my radio show and earmarked for a feature in *The Beacon* magazine.

Peter revealed how his first solo flight in a glider over Sussex changed his life for ever. Years later he became an RAF Group Captain and flew the lead aircraft in a flypast of 157 planes over Central London for the 50th Anniversary of the Battle of Britain. His service years also included the Queen, Prince Philip, whom he showed around the Brize Norton Airbase, Margaret Thatcher, John Major and the Beirut hostage John McCarthy.

His initial dream had been to become a fighter pilot but it just didn't happen that way.

"I flew a Jet Provost at 400mph but then they discovered I had a problem. I had really low blood pressure and could black out quickly at high speeds. Looking back now, it actually led to a career with a much wider variety of aircraft. I could fly Hercules and VC10s all around the world."

I was delighted to find that Peter was not self-opinionated in any way. Modestly, he revealed some great stories from his life. He had also been highly regarded as a very competent local councillor in the Shorwell area.

It had all began in a Varsity, a World War 2 bomber trainer, but he moved on to the very dependable Hercules. On his own admission, initially, he was a somewhat lazy co-pilot and just scraped in to achieve his rank of captain. Then his career suddenly took off – with him at the controls.

"My life changed very much for the better when I joined the 36 Squadron at Lyneham. I was always the first to volunteer when a new task came in and within a couple of weeks I was sent on my first long haul flight to Bahrain, which took 11 hours."

For three years Peter was transferred to the American Air Force – and the fee wasn't several million pounds, as he didn't play football.

"Because of wearing a different uniform, I was chosen to meet the new Governor of Arkansas, a certain Bill Clinton. I must admit, I never expected him to become President."

During his spell on the VC10s, Peter was once told he must pilot an aircraft and take two crews to Cyprus and await further instructions. His secret mission was to fly home the Beirut hostage John McCarthy, from Damascus. When they arrived back in England John was too stressed to talk, so Peter was told to talk to the media and was live on *News At Ten*.

Peter was also on a VC10 when Margaret Thatcher clocked up 1000 hours of flying time. Apparently, celebrations were held in mid-Atlantic. The mention of Maggie's successor, John Major, brought back scary memories. Peter was flying him back from the Gulf and he was keen to get back for a cabinet meeting the next morning. In foul weather conditions, the PM said he did not want to divert to Manchester. Somehow Peter got the plane into Heathrow despite the swirling wind and rain. It was the only plane to land that evening.

CHAPTER 35

Phill Jupitus

"JOHN, CONGRATULATIONS for being the first person to discover I was born on the Isle of Wight and to track me down," were the first words Phill Jupitus ever said to me. He seemed equally impressed when I told him he'd arrived in June, 1962, at St Mary's Hospital, Newport. The setting for our first meeting was the Tower Arts Centre in Winchester. I wasn't worried about impressing him – just happy to be there. There was so much I didn't know about his local roots.

In fact, four years after his birth, Phill's family moved to the mainland but he still had special memories to savour.

"I can always remember a huge flying boat cocooned out of the water," said Phill. This must have been one of the three giant Princess flying boats, of which only one ever flew. I had been lucky enough in 1952, while on school holidays, to see its maiden flight, with one of my schoolboy heroes, Geoffrey Tyson, at the controls.

There were also scrapbooks available of Phill's early days on the Island and, one in particular, pictured him with a rather suspect haircut. I think it was finally publicly exposed on *Room 101*. One of his greatest local followers was Ryde woodcarver Norman Gaches, his former step father. Norman actually gave me a few memories of young Phill.

"When Phill was about three he was rather an intense young lad with really piercing eyes. I can also always remember that haircut. He used to enjoy sitting on my knee. I would have reservations of him doing the same thing now. With our combined weights, I'd certainly need to check the chair first," said Norman.

Although Phill really broke through as a stand-up comedian, he was also asked to appear on other shows, due to his amazing knowledge of pop music. In the early days he was a tour manager for the Housemartins. He was not suited to this and was far more effective as their compere. He still had pictures of himself and group members sleeping on the floor of an Edinburgh university. One included Paul Heaton, who went on to Beautiful South, and Norman Cook, alias Fatboy Slim.

Before his Housemartins connection, Phill was a gifted illustrator and for a while worked in a Job Centre. He became semi-pro as Porky The Poet and was spotted by Billy Bragg, then the most successful indie recording artist on the scene. So he gave up the day job and toured with Billy. It didn't happen for him and he ended up as Billy's office boy for his record company. Then he joined the Housemartins as tour manager.

Eventually, he opted to try a career in comedy and was lucky enough to be on the pilot for TVs *Stand-Up Show*. His comedy success earned him a tour with Paul Weller – and then came *Never Mind The Buzzcocks*. The rest is history.

Phill has always been prepared to broaden his career path. Many were surprised when he became such a hit, as Edna Turnblad, in the celebrated West End musical *Hairspray*. He was a sensation – and I loved seeing him in the show. It was a long way from that Winchester gig in a round tower. Then came *Spamalot*, *Chitty Chitty Bang Bang* and *The Producers*. In another direction he's had a national radio show and is a long-term podcaster.

I've so enjoyed meeting him on numerous occasions and he always finds the time to be interviewed. Phill's such a great guy. What else would you expect from a true Islander?

CHAPTER 36

Keith Newbery

IN THE LATE summer of 1975 my father, Roy, came home from working at the *County Press* to reveal some amazing news. Two key members of the staff were leaving the CP to form their own newspaper, *The Isle of Wight Weekly Post*. Keith Newbery was to become the editor and Keith Huyton his deputy. The very next morning, when dad went back to

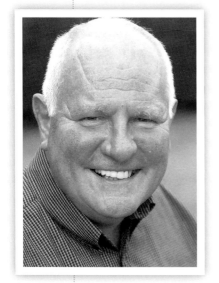

work, he took a message that I was interested in writing for them. I was invited to a meeting in a Sandown pub, an expected venue for journalists.

On Friday November 21, 1975, my life changed for ever. I was offered two regular weekly columns, *Stage Talk* and the *Post Sports Personality*. I went on to write in every issue until the paper closed in 1990.

Keith Newbery was in his element and the newspaper really took off and his previous employers saw a sudden drop in sales. It quickly became known for some brilliant pages of sport and, luckily, my showbiz column seemed to be popular.

Beyond any question of doubt, Keith could have become a top Fleet Street journalist. His love for his family and the Island meant he decided not to take it any further. He won national awards and sometimes was nominated among many of the London big guns. I know he was so honoured when the *Weekly Post* was mentioned among a list of famous British newspapers. When Margaret Thatcher visited the Island she wanted to know more about Keith and the *Weekly Post*.

Keith had a great sense of humour. He was a *Coronation Street* fanatic and one evening I rang him when the soap was on. We weren't in conversation for very long and I'd learnt my lesson. A month or two later I was sat watching, or more likely drooling over, one of my all-time favourites, Eartha Kitt, on an early evening chat show. Suddenly, when my phone rang, I was not too amused. It was Keith, getting his own back on me for ringing him while Corrie was on. I loved it.

During Larry Grayson's summer season at Sandown Pavilion I got to know him quite well and he asked me to bring a few friends to his dressing room, after an evening performance. I knew Keith was a great fan and we spent an hour in his company. Larry was in his dressing gown, with a cigarette holder and a glass of Wincarnis. Keith talked about it for weeks.

He was not really a showbiz fan but liked certain stars. He knew the scripts of every John Wayne movie and, amazingly, was so thrilled when I introduced him to Rod Hull.

If you were praised by Keith, you knew it was an honest opinion and a moment to treasure. I once hosted a Q & A at the Medina Theatre, Newport, following the movie *Scapegoat*. He was such a fan of Sheridan Smith, who was on the panel. His congratulations to me, at the end of the evening, have stayed with me ever since.

Once you were his friend, you were a friend for life. Although I worked for Keith for many years, our friendship was temporarily forgotten for about five hours when Havenstreet played Godshill in the Island's Village Cricket League. Friendships were renewed in the pub after the game – and that was how it should be.

If it had not been for Keith Newbery, I wouldn't have written this book or, indeed, any book. Those 5000 interviews would have never happened.

Sadly, he died much too soon in 2014. I feel privileged and honoured to have known him. Thankfully, I had managed to tell him on a few occasions during his life, that I owed it all to him.

CHAPTER 37

Tina St Clair

DURING MY EARLY YEARS at the *Weekly Post* I knew the perfect way to keep in with the editor, Keith Newbery, who has his own chapter opposite. My sixth *Stage Talk* article in the new local tabloid was on Island-based singer Tina St Clair. I knew she was a particular favourite of his and, subsequently, her picture was in more times than any other. I still remember the first time I ever introduced her to him. He never forgot it.

Tina was actually born in Australia and performed in a singing trio, with her two sisters. As the Hendry Sisters, they became a top Aussie singing act who had a Top Ten hit and appeared numerous times on television. Like others before her, Tina fancied a chance to work in Britain and sang her way over on the passage from Australia.

She quickly found work and sang in shows with stars like Vince Hill, Frankie Howerd and Charlie Drake. She also toured South Africa with Max Bygraves.

Tina was always in demand and she headed to the Island for summer season cabaret work and stayed for over 20 years. Her husband, John Ward, was a popular local photographer.

On one occasion, I went for a night out with Tina. She was in her Mini and I was in my Ford Popular. We hadn't fallen out. She was doing three gigs in the same evening and I went along to see how she managed it. With her didgeridoo in the Mini, there was no room for me. What a hectic night that was – and I didn't have to sing a note. I never told Mr Newbery much about it!

Tina was also so popular with Islanders and made regular appearances at local venues like the Ponda Rosa, Ryde Town Club and several conservative and social clubs. Strangely, she never had any problems in getting a guy up from the audience for her participation number. She also recorded an EP record, which sold well at her many gigs.

My favourite Tina St Clair story came in 1982. This was not three gigs in the same night. It was a 9000 mile trip for a 30 minute cabaret. She flew to Bermuda from Heathrow on the Tuesday to perform a cabaret spot the following evening at the Hamilton Princess Hotel, for just 40 people. After the seven hour flight she found out there was no pianist available who could read her band parts. Luckily, a former British bandleader, Terry Brennan, owned another local hotel and he came out of retirement to save the day. The night after her return home she was on stage at Warner's, Puckpool.

Eventually, Tina and John moved back to Australia to live in the outback, surrounded by animals. They were in their element. Such was her love for the Island, she came back for several summers to continue her cabaret work. I was thrilled to continue our long friendship and we met up on a few occasions. Thankfully, she could still really work an audience. Tina and John were also famous for their parties. I went to one and there were only two not drinking – Chris Cox and myself. We still reflect on that night, over a cup of coffee.

CHAPTER 38

Roy Barraclough

WHILE I WAS ENJOYING a 2017 Christmas special on the life of Les Dawson, watching part of the classic Cissie and Ada art gallery sketch, it took my mind back to 2001, when I first met up with famous actor Roy Barraclough, who was that very same Cissie. I went backstage at the Palace Theatre, Watford, to meet him.

Whenever I visited the Atherfield Bay Holiday Camp, I'd always noticed the picture of Roy Barraclough proudly displayed on the wall. In that Watford theatre dressing room he eagerly reflected on his days on the Military Road. To continue the story we need to

go back to 1962, when a young draughtsman decided to give up his job-for-life and head for the Isle of Wight.

Roy had gained experience in amateur shows but had a dream to become a professional entertainer. If he'd not taken that offer of his first professional job, a 16-week summer season in Atherfield, there might never have even been a Cissie and Ada routine or an Alec Gilroy in *Coronation Street*.

He told me, back in 2001." I learned such a lot from that first summer season and owe so much to the Newnham family, who owned the camp. They were so kind to me."

Roy quickly found his feet and as well as being the bar pianist he appeared in slapstick comedy routines and took the camp rambles. He revealed such happy memories.

"I used to sing riske songs and tell jokes in the bar but I had to keep an eye open for Mr Newnham, who frowned on anything too bold.

"The family had an old cottage near the top of the cliff for staff quarters and, after the camp closed for the night, we had a few wild parties. Mr Newnham would come over with a torch to see what we were up to and remind us we had an early start in the morning."

Roy certainly won many admirers during that season and admitted the camp's hairdresser, Angela, had a crush on him. Even when he became famous, he still received letters from those who remembered his days at Atherfield.

In 1987, several of the Newnham family flew up to Manchester to be guests on Roy's *This Is Your Life*. Fred Newnham, who owned the Atherfield camp, was not too well at the time but still made the effort to fly, for the first time in his life, to meet up with Roy on his special night.

I was lucky to have met Roy, who deservedly became an MBE, on a few other occasions. We had great fun at the Mayflower, Southampton, when he was one of the stars in *Santa Claus – The Musical*. Even then, he was still enthusing about his Island debut season. He told me: "It's quite amazing that my career started on the Isle of Wight and I will never forget my very first summer season."

For 25 years, millions followed Roy's exploits as Alec Gilroy in *Coronation Street*. Another chapter of his life that he enjoyed so much.

There is a possibility that a new kind of holiday centre could be built on the old Atherfield site. If so, it would be nice if they could remember Roy with a plaque or photograph. But, perhaps, not one of those statues that Ada tried to hide from Cissie in the art gallery!

CHAPTER 39

Les Snow

I GREW UP in East Cowes, at 1 Queens Cottages, in Old Road. Our next door neighbours were the Snow family. Early mornings, on schooldays, Les and I would often talk to each other in the outside toilets, across the gardens in the outhouse. Later I did play cricket with Les for East Cowes Saro but then we lost contact for many years.

Neither of us could have predicted what our future lives would lead to. We met up again over 50 years after those Old Road days, when I invited him on to my radio show. What a guest! I couldn't stop him talking and he'd achieved so much. What a memory, too. He could even remember the night I went sleep walking and jumped out of an upstairs window. My parents were so shocked when I called up to their bedroom, from the garden, in the early hours.

We reminisced about old neighbours, like the Blight family, and the nearby Saunders-Roe sports ground, where the wartime gun tower was still standing. Next door to our joined cottages was a reservoir, where Bob Cooper kept his pigeons.

Les was always such a naturally talented musician, particularly on the church organ. His parents were not wealthy and with no grants available in those days, he went into JS Whites Shipyard, as an engineering apprentice. Later he became a very gifted draughtsman. He went on to work for BHC and Vosper-Thornycrofts.

"One day I heard a guy at Vosper's say, 'I'll be staying around here until I get kicked out or retire.' I didn't want that and decided to do something about it," reflected Les.

At the age of 35, Les decided to train as a teacher at King Alfred's College, Winchester. What a shrewd move – and he came out with a degree. Then, as a full time teacher and later as a supply teacher, he worked at many local schools, including East Cowes Primary, Newport CE, Sandham and Niton. He went back to teach at his old Carisbrooke school, where he'd taken his GCSEs 44 years earlier. At one time, Les taught 120 pupils a week for music at various Island locations.

Being a schoolteacher was a real vocation for Les and he had so many letters of thanks and appreciation from very satisfied parents. He was liked wherever he went.

"Out of all the jobs I've ever done, teaching is my most satisfying. I treated them like my own and just told them to do their best."

Les, has played the organs at St James' Church and Whippingham Church for well over 40 years. He's been involved with the choirs at both and worked with the IW Cantata Choir and the Wootton Choral Society.

"I once was at Christ the King School and told them I had played the organ for 44 years at one church, 40 at another and ten at my first one. One boy told me I must be 94 years old."

A few facts you may not know about our Les. He danced the haka in New Zealand with the Maoris, has a four and a half octave vocal range and a huge lung capacity, which means he can disco dance for three hours. He once took five cricket wickets in six balls, has a golf handicap of eight and gives talks to passengers on cruise ships. More recently, he played the organ in Sydney Cathedral.

On my last visit to Old Road, our old outside toilets were still standing. It must be a listed building. There were no plaques on the doors, either, saying John Hannam and Leslie Snow first sat here and talked!

CHAPTER 40

Raymond Allen

Michele Dotrice and Ray

I'D SEEN Ryde's Raymond Allen long before he became so famous for writing *Some Mothers Do 'Ave 'Em*. I'd watched an outstanding Island Schools relay team who competed in the Hampshire Schools Athletic Championships. I knew three of them – Trevor Kings, 'Golly' Galton and Rod Nicholls. I never even remembered their fourth member but I knew he was slim and very fast. Raymond Allen was his name. Yes, it shocked me when Ray first told me. The only time he's run fast since then, was when he fled from an amorous Frankie Howerd.

When I first got to know Ray I found it hard to believe he had written so many marvellous scripts for Frank Spencer. Then, gradually, I realised just how clever and witty he was.

I could visualise the story he told me of when he was writing some scripts for the BBC but did not have a telephone in his Haylands home. He had to use the public one in the village. There would be a restless queue outside the box waiting for him to finish reading the scripts.

Ray had joined the *Ryde Times* as a trainee reporter and was always looking for a scoop – but was hardly likely to find one in births, marriages and deaths. On one occasion he had the unenviable task of going to the home of a football referee, who had just died. He was sent to talk to his widow.

"I nervously waited outside before I got the courage to knock the door. When I asked her if she would mind talking about her husband she seemed very friendly and asked me into the front room to see him. There he was sat in a chair with a newspaper over him and I was shocked by her lack of respect for her dearly departed. I was even more shocked when he sat up and asked for a cup of tea. Then she told me I was in the wrong house. It was next door," said Ray.

Away from Frank and Betty, Ray has always created many of his own personal comedy situations. I can reveal a few.

Once at Ryde Esplanade railway station he silenced a carriage load of people, who were clearly shocked. A friend asked him where he was going that afternoon.

Ray replied at the top of his voice: "I'm off to Shanklin Theatre to see *The Boyfriend*." It's rumoured one or two guys in the carriage moved swiftly away.

So many of us love his eccentricity. He once spotted a guy he didn't want to see, about to knock on his door – and he'd already seen Ray at the upstairs window. He answered the front door and, on the spur of the moment, invented a story that he was just off to the mainland. The man then offered to take him to the end of Ryde Pier. Ray was snookered. So he was taken to the end of Ryde Pier and actually got the ferry over and returned on the same one.

My late wife, Heather, once saw him in Newport High Street. He told her he'd been all the way to Southsea to buy chocolate at Thornton's. They were stood opposite their Newport store, which he knew nothing about.

What a gifted writer. In Britain 17 million regularly watched his show and a Christmas Special was seen by 23 million. Ray's such wonderful company, too.

CHAPTER 41

Mark King

IT WAS THE LATE summer of 1980 when I received a tip-off that a new chart group was actually practising at Ryde's Carousel Club, before their debut British tour. Nearby, late holidaymakers were whizzing around the go kart track and construction workers on the new Tesco site were toiling in the heat. The group, who included three Islanders, were called Level 42. It was the first time I'd met Mark King and we've talked on numerous occasions since then. I had seen him on stage before we met, with our own Pete Cotton Sound and local holiday camp bands.

My first real in-depth interview with Mark came a year or two later at the Gurnard Marsh home of his lovely parents. I have always been thrilled by the success of Islanders and, in Mark's case, he become one of the most influential bass players in the world, with a unique style that earned him the name of 'thunder thumbs.' Years later, I'll never forget being in the capacity audience at Ryde Arena when Level 42 arrived on a darkened stage and all you could see was the lights on Mark's bass. What a night that was!

Mark's success with Level 42 could fill this book, with huge hit singles all around the world and fantastic stadium concerts. I also loved his solo albums, particularly *One Man*, which came out in 1998. In fact, he was their somewhat reluctant singer at first but he got to like it. The band, with Mark and Mike Lindup as the consistent driving forces, have continued to tour. Level 42 did take a break for several years.

When I met Mark in 1984 he had three prime ambitions. To move back to the Isle of Wight, to mould Level 42 into a consistent Top 20 band and to make inroads into the American market. It's no surprise that he achieved all three.

I still think the moment that Mark King really arrived was in the finale of the epic Prince's Trust Concert. The supergroup on stage contained Paul McCartney, Elton John, Eric Clapton, Mark Knopfler, Phil Collins, Tina Turner, Paul Young, George Michael, David Bowie, Mick Jagger and Mark. Paul, Elton and Tina were self-confessed Mark King fans. That was a long way from a local Warner's holiday centre.

Mark has been such a credit to the Island and has always been prepared to give something back. In more recent years he's helped local charities and been happy to give time and advice to our young people. I love his sense of humour. Particularly on the day I shocked him by running past his house, which is well off the beaten track, whilst he was gardening.

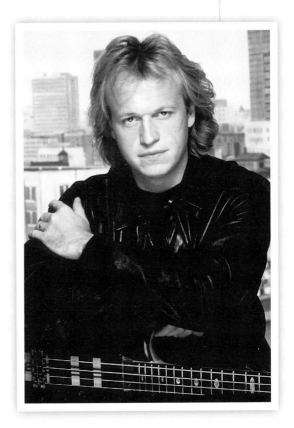

It's been a real fairytale. He was not a great pupil at Cowes High and the careers master laughed off his dream of becoming the best drummer in the world and sympathised with his mother.

"Despite no qualifications I decided to chase that dream. It wasn't going to happen delivering the milk in Gurnard. It was certainly scary but I just upped, put my drum kit in an old van and headed for London."

Eventually, world fame did come but as an innovative bass icon.

Several other Islanders have worked with Mark in different formations of Level 42. These include great talents like Boon and Phil Gould and Nathan King.

CHAPTER 42

Roy Harris

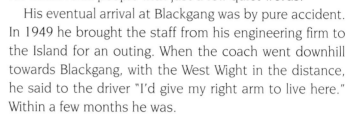

I FIRST MET Roy 'Pop' Harris in 1968, when I called on his St Catherine's Hotel at Blackgang. I was working for United Biscuits at the time. I'll never forget my friendship with him and his lovely wife Peggy. Roy was a man you instantly liked. I've never ever met a better person. He was a real gentleman. Softly spoken, modest and a real family man. He could relax people with just a few quiet words.

His eventual arrival at Blackgang was by pure accident. In 1949 he brought the staff from his engineering firm to the Island for an outing. When the coach went downhill towards Blackgang, with the West Wight in the distance, he said to the driver "I'd give my right arm to live here." Within a few months he was.

Roy had a stroke of luck. He saw an old dilapidated property in Blackgang Chine which was up for sale at £3500. I loved him relating this story.

"When I asked the agent, a man called Mr Wright, if there were others after it, he told me there were several. I didn't want a mortgage. Then he made the mistake of showing me a copy of a letter which had an offer of £2950 from someone else. I told him I'd have it at that price – and got it.

"It was really half of a house and half of that was rubbish. The first room I went into had six inches of water and a three foot hole in the outside wall. In another room I had to saw through ivy to get into it."

This was in December 1949 and Roy planned to open his hotel for the following summer. He managed to buy the second part of the house for £500 to complete his plan. One day they had a shock when a man turned up to see the room he'd booked for later in the summer. It wasn't there and there was no roof on it. For some reason he believed them – and was proved right.

Roy was told to buy some potatoes from a local guy called Ken. They met in a pub and the man was somewhat gruff and asked how many did he want. It frightened Roy a wee bit and he told him he didn't mind. Two days later a ton turned up and he had to bury them in the garden with straw.

St Catherine's might have started like a Basil Fawlty hotel but it quickly gained a superb reputation and business boomed. They had their own cinema with a real projection box and their daughter, Sally, even went around with ice creams. Heather and I were regularly invited out to see their movies. Wonderful nights and crab sandwiches in the kitchen before we went home.

Roy, who later became a very popular President of the IW Bowling Association, had a fund of stories. He picked one lady up from Ventnor Station, bundled her luggage into his car and tried to help her into the seat. She screamed: "I suppose you're going to rape me." He quietly told her that was not his intention and then found out she was a local lady, who wrote for the *Methodist Recorder*. She was waiting for her husband to pick her up and not a hotel guest.

On another occasion he picked up Lady Margaret Thorneycroft to take her to his hotel. His car had a soft top with holes in it. It rained and his esteemed passenger put her umbrella up. She asked him: "Mr Harris is this your only car?" Pop replied, "I only want one, mam."

CHAPTER 43

Megan Turner

SUNDAY, SEPTEMBER 6, 1998, was rather a special day for *John Hannam Meets*. Ann and Steve Turner brought their young baby daughter, Megan, into the studio and, luckily, she gurgled live on-air a couple of times. It proved a double celebration, as young Megan had been born in May, 16 weeks premature at just 1lb 6ozs. Initially, she was only given a 10% chance of survival. With her being the youngest person ever to appear on my radio show, it was indeed a time to celebrate.

John holding Megan

Megan came back on several occasions – and was never as quiet again. Her lovely mother Ann was not so keen to talk but I managed to charm her into it and she surprised everyone, particularly herself. Steve has never had a problem talking, either on or off the football field or sat in a studio with the red light on.

When Megan was born she could easily lay in dad's hand. Apparently, this did concern a few of his mates, who had seen him play in goal. In reality, Steve was such an inspiration. He always remained confident that all would be well and coped by taking pictures of her progress, thanks to the brilliant staff at St Mary's. The nurses made their own diary and kept it tied to the incubator, where she spent the first 10 weeks of her precious life. There was a message on the front of the book, which was written as if it was actually Megan. It read:" Will anyone who looked after me on my holiday here, please make an entry in the diary."

A few years later, when she came back on my show, Megan admitted she had read the diary.

"When I read it I got choked up because they obviously thought so much of tiny little me. I owe my life to them. They called themselves my 'nicu aunties', using the initials of their Neonatal Intensive Care Unit."

Megan was five when her parents told her the full story. They took her to an event promoting blood donors, as she was the perfect example of how blood helped her pull through. She needed it virtually every day of her hospital stay.

I sensed she would have something to add – and so it proved. "Dad was the smart gene, mum was the crazy gene and the sexy gene was down to the blood transfusions," said Megan.

Ann has an amazing box of memorabilia. They had to buy Megan a cat feeding bottle for her to take milk. During this delicate routine she also had a breathing tube in her mouth. The nappies were made from breast pads and the bootees were so tiny. At one time they had to shave her head to get into a vein. Ann still has the original hair.

Any fears that Megan might struggle in catching up were quickly quashed. Over the years she has sent me some of her writings and poems. I loved reading them – even though sometimes I wasn't on her wavelength.

The last time I interviewed Megan, her parents left us to it. I quickly picked up a few secrets. Ann had turned down a date with Steve on at least three occasions. Eventually, she relented and he gave her a bunch of carnations on their first date. I waited for the punch line from Megan.

"Now when dad buys flowers for mum, she wants to know what he's done or broken."

I love happy endings – and the lovely Megan Turner is a credit to everyone who helped her pull through. Pity about the hat!

CHAPTER 44

Michael Arnell

DURING MY 17 years at the helm of the Isle of Wight Amateur Theatre Awards I definitely heard a few sighs of pleasure when local matinee idol Michael Arnell came on stage. In fact, in his case, he was more of an after 7-30 idol, as Apollo Theatre matinees are quite rare. I saw him give some outstanding performances and after the final curtain they all ended in the same way – a cigarette, cup of tea and the bus ride home.

I'll never forget going to see him guest in a Cowes AODS production of *Jeffrey Bernard*

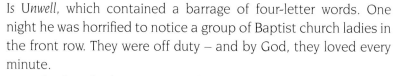

Is Unwell, which contained a barrage of four-letter words. One night he was horrified to notice a group of Baptist church ladies in the front row. They were off duty – and by God, they loved every minute.

Michael, with almost 200 productions to his name, is an actor who always make an impact. Amazingly, it was only because he was nagged by one of his school teacher colleagues, Frankie Goodall, at Kitbridge Middle, that he even took to the stage. Somehow, she talked him into playing Colonel Bully in *The Provoked Wife*.

"I don't know how she did it. I just didn't want to prance about on stage. I was no good at sport, had little co-ordination and could not even drive a car. Suddenly, I found I had a skill and loved it," admitted Michael.

Many years before his acting talents were discovered, he was so depressed with his boring job at the British Hovercraft Corporation. Friends, family and his local vicar realised how low he was and even chose a new career for him. He became a school teacher for around 30 years – and was a natural. Thousands of his ex-Island pupils will certainly vouch for that. The vicar's Save Michael Arnell Committee were an inspired group.

After qualifying at King Alfred's College, Winchester, he was snapped up at Kitbridge and spent five happy years there. Initially, to make ends meet, he became a summer bus conductor. At that time, although he hadn't started acting, his entertaining talents were becoming evident. On one occasion, to cheer up a bus load of wet and miserable holidaymakers returning to one of those Military Road camps, he had the downstairs group singing *Tipperary* and upstairs it was *Pack Up Your Troubles*. Not surprisingly, nobody wanted to get off.

For over 25 years Michael entertained so many young people at Solent Middle and 'Sir' was such a hit. He paid tribute to his head teacher Don Way, during one of our interviews.

"He understood what education was all about. Giving children responsibility for their own learning and to have a delight in it. You can do that by giving them responsibility and respect."

Michael's objective was to ensure the children looked forward to coming to school.

"Children don't mind how strict you are. They just don't like being nagged or shouted out. They also hate being bored, so you have to make teaching as wonderful as possible, by entertaining them with silly voices and anything to keep them on their toes." That was in 2003. I wonder if that still applies today?

Michael is a very proud family man and his wife, Margaret, and their two sons, Matthew and Morgan, have always given him great support.

Back to his thespian escapades. I loved it when his character confused line and lap dancing in *Nobody's Perfect*. In the *Last Of The Red Hot Lovers* he smoked pot and, somehow, he looked over 80 in *On Golden Pond*. That's what they call acting.

CHAPTER 45

Brian Munro and Ian Attrill

IN THE '70s the Island had two very gifted country singers, Brian Munro and Ian Attrill and I interviewed them both for the *Weekly Post*. They made local albums and were awarded silver discs by Tom Taylor, the owner of Peacock Records.

I was compering a show at the Ponda Rosa in 1977, which featured both singers, and was asked to come on during Ian's act to surprise him and let Brian present him with his silver disc.

Ian, who went blind in the '60s, has always had such a wonderful sense of humour. The first time I interviewed him I went to his home and interrupted his gardening to have our chat to promote his new album. He can talk for ever and at around 10-30pm I decided to head home. Then he surprised me.

"Thanks for coming John. Now I'm going to go back into the garden to finish my digging. The dark makes no difference to me," said Ian, with that well known beaming smile.

Ian's earliest musical influences were Frankie Laine, Jo Stafford and Big Bill Campbell.

"My first contribution to the local music scene was in the days of skiffle and talent contests at the Medina and Commodore. It was great fun and a group like the Niton Traders would turn up with seven guitarists, a washboard and tea chest bass, quickly followed by the Signal Box Five from Merstone," said Ian, whose first local country band was the Rustlers.

Later his search for a job for a blind person, within Social Services, led him to Hull where he got the job, met his wife, Pat, and began singing in the northern clubs. Eventually he moved back to the Island and performed again at local venues. In more recent years he has done so much valuable work for local churches.

Brian Munro was inspired by an *Oh Boy!* live show in Plymouth and after leaving national service came back home to Cowes and played in the local scouts skiffle group, alongside Alan Yarrington, Bruce Matthews and Laurie Turner.

"We got away with murder and we performed at places like the Princes Cafe, Gurnard," said Brian.

He then played guitar in the Medina City Jazz Band before forming his own group. The Brian Munro Trio appeared on Southern TV's *Home Grown*, compered by Dickie Davies.

Being a Cowes postman and working from 4am until 2pm were not ideal hours for a singer and one night he even fell asleep on stage. This led to him giving up for a while. It didn't last and he returned to help form the legendary Island country band, Union Pacific.

During the 1970 Pop Festival the band were playing at the Clarendon, Shanklin, and had gone down a storm. After the show they were complimented by an unknown American admirer, who was in the audience. His name was Kris Kristofferson. He also sang that night and performed some of the songs he was trying to get published, like *Me And Bobby McGee* and *For The Good Times*. That was a night to remember for Brian, who continued to sing at local venues for many years.

Brian Munro and Ian Attrill

CHAPTER 46

Michael Spiers aka Michael Jon

HAVE YOU HEARD to one about the local ladies hairdresser who once ran a mile in 4.27 minutes and a half mile in 1.59. He won 22 Island titles in only five years of athletics? It's all true, too.

That was the opening paragraph of an article I wrote for the *Weekly Post* in 1985. It was about the Island's former superstar athlete Michael Spiers, who went on to become Michael Jon, our most famous hairdresser of that period.

During my days as a middle distance runner I had certainly heard of the amazing Mike Spiers but, luckily, he'd already retired.

The mile was Michael's speciality. On the Island he was never beaten over that distance. His fastest time of 4.27 was recorded in a race at the JS Whites Sports Ground, Cowes.

He was an all-round athlete and during his career won the Island 100 yards, 220, 440, 880, mile and three miles. He also won our cross country championship and every javelin event he entered here.

Michael, who first came to the Island when his father was posted to Nodes Point on army duty, gave up running after five years of local competitions and was simply in a class of his own, with so much unfulfilled potential. At that time, the Island had never seen an athlete of his calibre. Rather shrewdly, he gave it up to pursue his career as a hairdresser and founded his famous Michael Jon hair salon. That led him to more success, in a completely different field. He spent 32 years in his Newport High Street shop. For several years he had another branch in Sandown. At one time, he had over 30 staff employed in his salons.

"I owe such a lot to athletics. It gave me a determination to get through," said Michael. That experience helped his business career flourish.

When I first met Michael, back in '85, it was the golden age of milers and 1500 metre stars. Was he envious of their success and wealth?

"I have great admiration for people like Coe and Cram but am not envious. I didn't have the same outlook on life to reach that stage. My purpose wasn't strong enough. I just enjoyed it and had a night out with the boys if I felt like it."

Amazingly, when the Smallbrook running track was opened he made a special comeback for his sons, who had never seen him run. Without running at all for 17 years, he decided to enter the 440 in the new venue for the Island championships. He'd actually won this event 21 years earlier. He came out of retirement, with no training at all, and came second. Quite an achievement.

Many years earlier Michael had made the headlines in the French press. Studying to be a hair stylist in Monte Carlo, he came second in a South of France cross country race. The Monaco club were delighted and he won his colours. The newspaper banner headline read "Le Monegasque Spiers."

The last time I interviewed Michael was in late 2017. As we walked out of his house, I asked him a question that I'd pondered over since the '70s, after discovering that Island-born Jeremy Irons grew up in St Helens. Where was the house?

"If you look just over there, you can see the roof," said Michael. Another mystery solved. We were that close to it. Jeremy once told me he had a dream to buy it back.

CHAPTER 47

Celia Imrie

I FIRST MET Celia Imrie in 1983, at the unlikely setting of the Binstead Community Centre. I was invited to come and interview her by a guy called Fred Smith, who I quickly realised was rather besotted by the beautiful actor. He'd invited her to a special sponsored badminton event. At that time, Celia was probably best known as Bergerac's financial friend, Marianne, in the hit TV series, and had just emerged as the delightfully quaint Miss Babs, in the Victoria Wood shows.

Celia was staying with friends at Bonchurch but quickly told me her immediate plans included buying a house on the Island. Within a year or two that dream came true and she moved into a cosy little house in St Mary's Road, Cowes.

We became friends and she appeared numerous times on my radio show, which excited quite a few who worked there. I used to pick her up and drop her back after the show. On one occasion she asked if we could go via the Newport postal sorting office. There was a parcel to pick up, as she had been off the Island working. Celia was not amused. It turned out to be a London parking fine.

I well remember going to her home to see her newly born son Angus. There was great excitement. Nearly 20 years later I was interviewing Celia at her new Cowes address, about 50 yards from former BBC newscaster and presenter Kenneth Kendall, who is featured later in this book, and was suddenly aware of a tall person standing behind me. I suddenly felt very old – it was Angus. He was then a burgeoning actor and had already been seen in the *Kingdom* television series. Since then, there's been *The Hollow Crown*, *Father Brown* and Josh Archer in *The Archers*. His father, the late Benjamin Whitrow, was also a brilliant actor.

Celia has been one of Britain's most successful actors of the past 40 years. She has always found quality parts to play, throughout her long career, that have suited her age perfectly. It's almost easier to say what she hasn't been in. My favourites include *The Riff Raff Element*, *The Love Punch*, *The Best Exotic Marigold Hotel*, *What We Did On Our Holidays* and, of course, *Calendar Girls*. When the latter movie was showing at local cinemas, Celia rang to say she was on the Island and would be happy to be interviewed. It may not be a surprise to you that the subject of ice buns came up! Apparently, she still had one in her office. Was it one of the 'bigger buns?'

When Heather and I were shopping in Sainsbury's she would often ask "would you like a Celia Imrie for later?" Yes – that was an ice bun!

When Celia shopped in Cowes, it was at Hewitts. This was a small high street grocery store next to the post office. It seemed that wherever the owner, Roger Cross, was, most likely in his office, he quickly ended up in the shop when Miss Imrie called in. Years earlier, Uffa Fox had been a regular customer.

Celia loves the Island and she always told me her shoulders dropped and she felt so relaxed the minute she got on the ferry, fresh from another major acting role. She did arrange Literatours of the Island. I joined one of her coach tours and thoroughly enjoyed it.

Following her amazing autobiography, *The Happy Hoofer*, Celia is now a best selling novelist.

I'm so glad I went to that Binstead badminton event back in '83. Thanks to Fred Smith.

NB. *The picture was taken at the Binstead Community Centre in 1983.*

CHAPTER 48

Morris Barton

I KNEW MORRIS BARTON long before he became the most famous person on the Isle of Wight. When he first joined the *County Press* he was an apprentice linotype operator to my late father, Roy. When dad revealed stories from work, Morris was often mentioned. They were both strong Labour supporters and staunch union members.

Ironically, the last time I ever interviewed Morris he told me just how brilliant my father was and that he could have made a real fortune in Fleet Street. Apparently, he never made a mistake, when typing copy into hot metal, and was so fast with his fingers.

My long friendship with Morris was not political in any way. I've never had an allegiance to any party, so I enjoyed the other side of his life, including music and sport. I had him on IW Radio's *John Hannam Meets* three times and interviewed him twice on television.

Once I had Morris and Jack Douglas on the same live radio show. The night before I took Morris and his lovely wife, Marcia, to Jack's show at Shanklin Theatre. I remember it well – and the free ice creams, courtesy of the IW Council.

When Jasper Carrott and Jo Brand came to perform at local concerts, I was the mole who suggested the mention of a certain Morris Barton might get a laugh. It worked a treat and, of course, he enjoyed every minute.

Morris did certainly not enter politics for money. From 1969 to 2000 he never received any salary for his council work. He was certainly no back bencher, either. He told me once: "I was always someone who wanted to do things. I was not interested in just sitting there for the sake of getting a chain or a badge."

Quite rightly, Morris was always proud of being a boy from Pan Estate. When he left the Labour party he became the Liberal councillor for Pan.

I always had an ambition to get Morris and his old neighbour, Terry Perkins, who became world famous singer Craig Douglas, on the same show. That eventually happened on a my TV12 chat show. They were both 'Barton Boneheads' from Pan Close. Didn't they do well!

Morris, who sadly died in 2017, always existed on just a few hours sleep. He was always up early to listen to the world news and BBC Radio's 5 *Live*. After his retirement from major Island politics, he would watch 10 television news shows every day. Once, when I popped in, he was watching a French station.

I still think Morris would have made a great local MP. He was so fanatical about the Island and its people – and he was one of us. I'm sure Steve Ross would have liked that.

The last time I ever interviewed Morris I asked him for his thoughts on that very subject.

"I regret I did not stand for Parliament when I had the opportunity. We had small children at the time and I was financially strapped."

Marcia was the wind beneath his wings and I love the story of how they met. It was at a Woolworth's dance at the Grantham Hotel, Cowes. He went there late in the night, purely to pick up his mother and he suddenly noticed a stunning blonde. Within minutes, he was dancing with her.

How did Marcia remember it? "It was late and I saw this good looking rather dark skinned guy (he'd just got back from a holiday in Spain) who I thought had a touch of arrogance about him."

Rumours suggest, he proposed to her on a bus to Wootton. Their song was *You've Got A Friend* – and they were together for 51 years.

CHAPTER 49

Les Payne

NEWPORT-BORN Les Payne is probably the unluckiest songwriter the Island has ever produced. He wrote so many stunning songs for both himself and his '70s band, Mainland. Some, like I *Can't Help To Feel The Love* and *No Money*, were records of the week on Radio 1. If only a major star had recorded one of his songs, Les' career might have been so different. He wouldn't have performed over 6000 gigs, that's for sure. He was so near to a major breakthrough on several occasions.

Les always had a dream of making the big time and this continued until his sad death in 2017. There were memorable moments in his 50-year career as a professional singer. It all began when he became a member of the Priory Boys Choir. Then came a Newport skiffle group and also the chance to sing during Johnny Vincent's breaks at the Hotel Ryde Castle. Later, after he'd moved to the mainland, Les and his group toured with Leo Sayer and supported name acts like Genesis, Mott The Hoople and Free. He was even seen in a series of television commercials.

He was so honoured, in 1991, to become the first unknown to win a Harp Beat Rock Award. He followed Tom Jones, Simon and Garfunkel, The Troggs and Elvis Presley. "Who the hell is Les Payne?" That was a frequently asked question in rock circles. In fact, it made world news. He was seen on all our major British TV channels and even stations in Australia, Russia and Bulgaria. There was a queue of famous radio presenters clambering to interview him. These included Tony Blackburn, James Whale, Chris Tarrant, Johnny Walker and Simon Bates.

Diana Ross saw Les on breakfast television and invited him to her private party. They were seen dancing cheek to cheek. Sadly, all the publicity happened so quickly and Les did not have a record deal to capitalise on it.

Les had endured a problem several years earlier when his brilliant solo single, I *Can't Help To Feel The Love*, released by RCA, had 127 plays on Radio 1. It was destined for the pop charts but a three-day-week and a vinyl strike sabotaged its chances.

During his life, Les had such a reputation for helping others. He was always so keen to help young performers and encouraged many to use his back garden studio. I interviewed him there on one occasion. On the same day I met famous songwriter and record producer John Schroeder, who worked on records by Helen Shapiro and Status Quo. We all had a meal at Les' home near High Wycombe.

Les was also in awe of his young Island cousin, Keir Hicks, a sensational guitarist. I was honoured to see them work together. Keir was 19 at the time.

I met Les on numerous occasions and whenever he came back to the Island he always popped in to see us. Over the years I have personally taken comfort from the lyrics of some of his songs, particularly *Missing You*.

During his life, Les Payne achieved so much more that a few one-hit wonders I have met. Over 6000 gigs was a marvellous achievement. As a fellow-Islander, I was proud and honoured to attend his remarkable funeral at the Chiltern's Crematorium. They were even sitting on the floor. Locals had never seen crowds like it. When the coffin arrived, there was several minutes of clapping and cheering all around the hearse. He deserved it all – and had given so much happiness to his fans.

CHAPTER 50

Colin Smith

I CAN REMEMBER going to the East Cowes Methodist Church Sunday School in the early '50s and listening to Miss Hollis tell us about two incredible brothers from Yarmouth, Colin and Stan Smith, who had sailed the Atlantic in 1949, in their 20 foot boat *Nova Espero*. At the end, I went to view their autographs that she had collected. Much to my surprise, she gave them to me.

Fifty years later I actually had Colin live on my radio show. Sadly, Stan had died by then. I was completely transfixed by their story. It was long before computers and health and safety. Their 43-day adventure was undertaken without a radio, lifejackets or trendy

Musto yachting gear. They even wore sports jackets and flannels, cooked on a Primus stove, took far less fresh water than they should have done and dried out their soggy sleeping bag every day.

"It was just an adventure for us. We had both come through the war and were full of life. We were confident in the boat we had built ourselves. If we were scared at all, it was over the possibility of our own fallibility but we thought we would make it," revealed Colin.

They did take a portable radio to help them track an exact longitude. They couldn't even get a weather forecast. It's probably still at the bottom of the Atlantic, covered in barnacles. They left Dartmouth, Nova Scotia and headed for Dartmouth, England.

"We sat on the cabin floor, which had a three foot six headroom, with the stove between our knees and held on to the saucepan or kettle with one hand and the boat with the other."

They had such a shock when a huge whale emerged just a few yards from their boat. Thankfully, it was not a Jonah moment and Colin was still around to recall the story. On one occasion, they had real fresh food. Colin was on night watch when a garfish, who must have felt sorry for them, dived on board.

Five days out a large ship hailed our intrepid brothers and asked where they were heading. When they shouted "England" there was some confusion. "Did you say New England?," came back the reply. They seemed surprised but Colin and Stan assured them that all was well and headed for home.

A miracle happened in mid-Atlantic. Colin had one foot on the tiller and one holding the main sheet and when Stan arrived with a plate of food he became distracted. The boat suddenly gybed and he went over the side with no lifejacket or harness. I loved it when Colin recalled the story.

"When I came up for the first time I'd never seen our little boat sailing on the Atlantic. Stan was looking for me and I can remember shouting how marvellous she looked from the sea. I probably did it to reassure him I was okay.

"For several minutes I only saw our boat for a few seconds at a time and then it disappeared in the huge waves. Stan was attempting to gybe her around to try and pick me up. Then by some real good fortune she was right above me and I managed to hold on and climb aboard."

Colin and Stan had a fantastic reception in Dartmouth. They soon sailed back home to Yarmouth and thousands were there to mob our Island super heroes, who were shocked by their sudden fame. Their 3000 mile journey made oceanic history and worldwide news.

Colin died at the wonderful age of 96, in early 2018.

CHAPTER 51

Wilf Pine

BACK IN 1976 when I was writing my *Stage Talk* column in the IW *Weekly Post*, I received a letter from a guy called Wilf Pine, who lived in Binstead. I readily accepted his lunch invitation, as I certainly knew his name and local reputation. We hit if off from that first meeting and remained friends for over 40 years. At that time, he was promoting shows at the Oasis, Ryde, and the acts included Sheer Elegance, The Troggs and Geno Washington and the Ram Jam Band. In the '60s, Wilf had brought huge bands to the Island, including Amen Corner, Black Sabbath and Yes.

It wasn't until 2003 that I discovered the real Wilf Pine story. He'd always told me I didn't need to know. Heather and I went to Eastbourne to meet crime writer John Pearson, who had just written the life of Wilf Pine, in a book called *One Of The Family – The Englishman And The Mafia*. Wilf was also there and I teased him about the fact I now knew a lot more about him.

There was an interesting follow-up to this story. A few months after the book was published, I interviewed Elkie Brooks on Wimbledon Common. She knew I was from the Island and asked me if I knew Wilf Pine, as she'd just read the book on him and was dying to meet him. She became so excited when I told her he was a good friend of mine. I set it all up and a few weeks later we all met up in a village pub near Salisbury. I interviewed them both for my radio show – and people still talk about it.

Wilf grew up in Oakfield and his Island life was far from easy. He ended up at an approved school in Northumberland, which made him a very different person. His subsequent life included a close friendship with the Kray family, being accepted by the Mafia and enjoying the glamour and rewards of working with rock groups like Black Sabbath and Stray. He also produced records, including a great contemporary album by Elkie Brooks.

In his early days he was a bouncer at Island nightclubs and later brought top pop groups to the end of Ryde Pier, including The Tremeloes, Amen Corner and The Move. He also got The Cherokees a single, called *Candle In The Wind*, on Parlophone, which they recorded as Wilfred.

Wilf was often called to London for "heavy work", which involved debt collecting and doing virtually anything for money. He worked for Don Arden and there are legendary stories that still circulate.

He adored my late wife and when she was diagnosed with cancer we received the biggest bunch of flowers we'd ever seen. I have never forgotten that gesture from a man with a heart of gold. We were from different worlds but loved each other with real affection.

John Pearson wrote this in his 2003 book. "Wilf is one of the most respected villains in Britain today." I liked to think of him, more affectionately, as a hoodlum.

I'm so pleased I was brave enough to have turned up for that lunch back in '76.

Amazingly, Wilf went from working as a relief dustman in Ryde to driving a Rolls Royce Silver Cloud and having his own glamorous office in London's Mayfair. He touched the hearts of so many people. At his 2018 funeral service, Elkie Brooks sang live and Fred Dinenage delivered the eulogy. Billy Murray, who played DS Don Beech in *The Bill* for ten years, also attended, as did friends from the Island. You can have a brilliant funeral – and Wilf's was certainly that.

CHAPTER 52

Barney Powell

LONG BEFORE I knew Barney Powell I always visited his famous Barney's Emporium, when I was in Shanklin. In summer, the visitors swarmed around his shop to view the complete rubbish in the windows, which all had very funny cards attached to them. The only decent things he had in the shop were quality binoculars, which were his speciality.

Barney had spent 50 years in showbusiness and was still doing local hotel and theatre gigs. In summer, he lived in his ramshackle home in Luccombe, called Manana, and in the winter he headed for the Canary Islands and worked his passage by doing cabaret on board the ship.

After initially playing the drums, rather badly, he switched to the xylophone and did the same act for well over 30 years. I loved his stories about playing the Windmill. Long before moving to the Island, he played there for ten winters. Other unknowns he worked with included Bruce Forsyth and Arthur English.

"At the Windmill I was never discovered, I was rumbled. Bruce Forsyth actually gave me a pair of his dancing shoes, which I still wear in my act," said Barney.

When I went to Bruce's home to interview him, I mentioned Barney Powell and he remembered him. Once I was stood in the wings at Shanklin Theatre with Roy Hudd, watching Barney on stage. Roy, a legendary musical hall historian, had never seen an act like it before. He became quite emotional.

In 1932 Barney came to the Island to appear with Clarkson Rose in *Twinkle*, on Shanklin Pier. Altogether, Barney enjoyed 12 summer seasons at the theatre. For several years Tommy Trinder was their principal comedian. Almost opposite, at the Summer Theatre, which is now an amusement arcade, the opposition Sunshine Company presented the virtually unknown Arthur Askey for eight summers. Rumours suggest each theatre manager looked at their opposition with binoculars – to see how many were going in.

During his long career, Barney, who appeared in 33 summer seasons all over Britain, supported some of the greatest stars of the period. He once told me: "When George Best used to score for Manchester United you didn't always see the person who passed the ball. Artists like myself, pass the ball, so to speak, to the big names at the top of the bill."

Barney opened his emporium in 1955 and many famous stars, who played at the nearby Shanklin Theatre, popped in to see him. Dick Emery was a regular visitor and others included Tommy Trinder and Norman Vaughan. When harmonica wizard Larry Adler played Sandown Pavilion, Barney went backstage to see him. Larry remembered him from a Brighton show they had both appeared in.

The first time I went into the shop to interview him it was 30 minutes to savour and he was in great form. Some ladies were testing his quality binoculars and he called out to them "ladies you might see a bit more if you take the lens caps off." Then a guy asked if he could take them outside to test. "Yes, certainly. I'm wearing my plimsolls," quipped Barney.

Quite rightly, he was also so proud of the money he had raised for the Shanklin Cottage Hospital. It was not far off £2000.

CHAPTER 53

Paul Armfield

I'VE ALWAYS enjoyed the talents of Paul Armfield. He's a great singer/songwriter and musician, with several superb albums to his name. He was also an outstanding manager at Newport's Waterstones book store. In more recent years he's proved just the person to revive the fortunes of our Quay Arts Centre.

We first met up in 1986 and it was all due to a lovely guy called Pete Wragg, who ran The Tavern Bar, at Ventnor's Royal Hotel. It was a favourite haunt of both musicians and cricketers. Pete rang me with an invite to attend a rehearsal night of a new Island band called Bobby I Can Fly. The venue was the old Julises nightclub, which at that time was rather damp. Their personnel was Duncan Jones, Mark Wozencroft, Carl Grant, Dave Baker and Jamie Shirlaw, with Paul on bass.

He gave me a great quote for my *Weekly Post* column: "I was vicious and needed calming and Duncan was mellow and needed beefing up."

Paul had come from the punk era and Duncan was more used to singing Simon and Garfunkel songs. I still treasure an old chrome cassette with their London demo sessions. My favourite track, *So Much For Hollywood*, was released, locally, around the new millennium, on a Vaguely Sunny CD called *Isle Of Wight Rock Anthology*.

Their guiding light was Robin Britten from Bembridge, who had previously worked with Craig Douglas, the Hollies and Gene Pitney. They should have made the big time.

Paul was the manager of Waterstones, previously Ottakers, for around 20 years, before he was made redundant. It was his brainchild to hold special evenings to present both local and famous authors and performers. I have fond memories of interviews, in his tiny upstairs office, with David Bellamy, Patrick Moore and Sally Farmiloe. I also introduced his evening with Island-born Fleet Street journalist Brian Scovell.

On one special night, both Paul and myself were very unhappy. There was a shop full of people waiting for an appearance by Bear Grylls – and he just never turned up. I've never watched one of his TV shows since that night.

Paul has made some quite brilliant albums, using so many talented Island musicians. *Songs Without Words* was his first and he's never looked back. His unique voice, phrasing and personal songs can be quite mesmerising. His local concerts are always sold out.

Since leaving the book trade, he's become a successful wandering troubadour. He regularly tours France, Germany, Holland, Italy and Austria. In fact, he has fans all over Europe. His British stage appearances include Glastonbury.

On one of our many interviews, I asked Paul if he had ever wanted to be a famous star – and was not surprised at his reply. "I've always really just wanted to make music and let people hear my songs and appreciate them. In my early days I had an unhappy spell when I just wasn't playing music."

Some will still remember Paul in his days with the Dance Preachers, Chuff Train Stompers and CRAP. The latter band, comprised of Chas Phillips, Roland Jones, Adam Kirk and Paul. Hence the name. Paul loved writing songs with Adam, the son of the late local footballer Mick Kirk, and was so thrilled a few years later to see that Adam was playing the guitar for Joan Baez. He also played guitar at Glastonbury for Tanita Tikarim. Paul and Adam have still played together and collaborated on songs, when the opportunities have arisen.

As well as making albums and touring Europe, Paul also manages Newport's Quay Arts Centre, where he's always keen to try new ideas.

CHAPTER 54

Graham Daish

THE LAST TIME I interviewed Graham Daish, one of the Island's most successful football managers of all time, it was far away from Whippingham or Smallbrook Stadium, where he'd enjoyed making history with local teams East Cowes Vics and Ryde Sports. It was actually in Wiltshire, where he'd moved to with his lovely wife Rose. We even had morning coffee in Salisbury Cathedral.

Graham won league titles with four different local clubs, East Cowes Vics, Newport, Ryde Sports and West Wight. The success he had at the Vics is still remembered by many, including yours truly, as his greatest sporting achievement. The often called 'Cinderella club,' from near Whippingham Church, had been in the shadow of both Newport and Cowes for many years. Suddenly they became the Island's top team and went on a 74-game unbeaten run, to take two consecutive Hampshire League titles. It was the most successful spell in the club's history.

"Particularly in our first championship season there was a lot of money being thrown about at other clubs. My boys paid a £1 to play. We had a great side of all-Island players and I wouldn't have changed any of them," said Graham, during one of our many interviews.

At one time, he was the envy of most other south coast non league managers. Having a front line of Mark Deacon, Steve Greening and Gareth Williams was an invincible combination. They just tore teams apart. Those three hit the headlines but it was such a great all round side, with others like Gerry Shaw, John Hazell, John Simpkins, John Watson and co. I still feel so privileged to have covered the Vics during their epic seasons. There were some great evening away trips, which included a late night call for chips, at the 'greasy spoon' kiosk at Portsmouth Harbour.

As a footballer himself, Graham had been a late developer. He couldn't get into the Priory Boys team but did make his world debut playing for JS Whites, as a full back. By the way, he certainly wasn't a flying wing back! Later he signed for the Vics before moving to Brading.

During his days as a manager he had a great supporting cast of quality coaches, including John Carragher and Roger North. I want to pick out some of 'Daisher's' greatest moments.

Obviously that 74-game unbeaten run must take pride of place but he had some other notable achievements. In one close season he signed Barry Allen, Chris Cheverton and Tony Grimwade for the Whippingham club. Then he tempted Nick Holmes, one of Southampton's 1976 Cup Final winning team, to play for the Vics. That surprised a few. For other local clubs, he won an Island League title for Newport Reserves, a Wessex League championship for Ryde Sports, they were fourth from bottom when he took over, and he led West Wight to several trophies during his six years at Camp Road.

Graham had worldwide success. In 1974 the family had moved to Africa for a few years and, subsequently, he managed Nchanga Rangers from Zambia, who fielded two internationals. They played in front of crowds of 8000. He only gave up because he couldn't get his ideas across to his players. Many didn't understand English or Isle of Wight!

Footballers have never been known for their loyalty but Graham was so lucky in this direction. So many of his players remained with him. John Watson was the perfect example. At 17, he became a 'Daish babe', after moving from BHC, and he stayed with the boss for the rest of his long career.

Graham enhanced the reputation of Island football and local players. No other manager has come close to his achievements.

CHAPTER 55

Malcolm Lawrence

FITTING THE LIFE of Malc Lawrence into one chapter is virtually impossible. It includes the Rolling Stones, the La Babalu Club, midnight streaking down Ryde's notorious Beaper Shute, being an English Schools sprinting champion, winning Havenstreet CC's single wicket competition, playing rugby for the Hurricanes and selling van loads of crisps. It's never ending. He played soccer with John Sissons and became the noisiest after dinner speaker on the Island.

Before coming here in the '60s, he was a drummer. His band, Lee Allen and the Sceptres, supported acts like Brian Poole, Joe Brown and Screaming Lord Sutch. At the Cellar Club in Ealing, he often sat in with the unknown Rolling Stones, alongside Mick Jagger, Brian Jones, Keith Richards and co.

Could our Malc have been the fastest sprinter for his age in England? He won a 100 yard sprint at the White City.

He once told me: "At that time I clocked under 11 seconds for the 100 yards. Now it takes me two hours and a bus ride."

Malc, such fun to be with, has a fund of stories. My favourite concerns the night he was stopped by the police, as he ran naked down Beaper Shute, from La Babalu, where he was the resident DJ. It must have been a dare. When the policeman got out, he was heard to say: "Oh, it's you Malc. We'll see you later at the club." He carried on and completed his midnight streak. Rumours suggest, at that time, the local coppers knew where to go for an early morning drink.

For years he was a popular after dinner speaker at Island sporting functions - and he had a great party trick. He would sneak in some old crockery and hide it under the top table. When he got up to speak, he would smash all the old crockery and waiters would come flying out of the kitchen, thinking it was their best china. It never failed.

Malc was a close friend of the late Keith Newbery – and they got up to a few tricks. Keith once suggested that Malc had got so much better at cricket that he was able to take the front and back labels off his bat.

Apparently, on his arrival day, he eventually found the Havenstreet bus, his parents had moved there a couple of years earlier, after being sidetracked at the Bow Bars.

"After London, the village seemed like bliss, so I decided to stay. I had no friends and found work hard to get. My only wild living was bingo with the local pensioners."

Malc loved his rugby and played for the Hurricanes, following a chance meeting with Emile Rouby. Yes, it was in a pub. In his first game for the seconds he got three tries and eventually went on to skipper the team.

A born salesman, he was also a very successful salesman for Reliant Foods – and was their crisp king.

In more recent years, Malc has been such a faithful follower of Ventnor Cricket Club and enjoys their Southern League matches. When Malc and Keith Newbery were together it was a real double act. This had begun on 'The Hump' at Havenstreet and continued at Steephill and Newclose.

They both predicted a brilliant future for Ventnor's overseas player Travis Head. He was an Australian and spent a season at the club. Since then he's played for the Aussies and Yorkshire.

CHAPTER 56

Colin Carmichael

THE DAY I WENT to Medina High School to see their production of *Fiddler On The Roof*, I came out enthusing about the superb performance of Colin Carmichael, who played the lead role of Tevye. From that inspiring performance, I was certain he could become a professional actor. It was beyond my wildest dreams that I would later see him in *The Bill*, *EastEnders*, *The Dectectorists* and some of the most successful television commercials in Britain.

Colin was actually one of the original two runners seen in the 118 118 television commercials. He spent 10 years appearing in them and they were filmed all around the world.

He told me during one of our many interviews: "They were a bit tough with all that running about. I was never fit at school but tried to look cool in my shell suit."

Since the 118 commercials, he's been seen in many others including *Go Compare*, B&Q, *Carling* and *Belvita*. During the 10 years of 118 he was never recognised, due to the huge moustache and that horrendous wig. He was not even noticed in his local, the White Horse at Whitwell.

Colin is so clever with his facial expressions and body movements. He has a real gift for comedy. He's also a very shrewd actor. Basically, he's a theatre maker and ran his own company for many years. Being so much in demand, at the most lucrative time for television commercials, he was able to fund his own stage projects. They also bought him a house and a few vintage cars.

I love the story of when Colin was walking by a huge poster of himself, advertising Carling, and he suddenly realised Nigel Planer, Neil from *The Young Ones*, was giving him a double take. In that instant, he was flattered to be recognised.

In an episode of *The Bill*, as Johnny Mace, he threatened a copper with a shotgun and was involved in several powerful scenes. Actor Eric Richard, who played Sgt Bob Cryer, once told me how much he was impressed with Colin, in that storyline. The *EastEnders* chance came from a surprise phone call. He played a hired date for Kim, which ended with disaster for his role of Sinclair, a well spoken geek with a racist outlook.

In an early performance of A *Midsummer Night's Dream*, which eventually toured the world, Colin, as Quince, got so excited that he fell off the high stage and couldn't get back up. The guy playing Bottom wouldn't come out of character to help him back on stage. During his career he has also appeared in other classics like *As You Like It*. There have been a few movies, far removed from Shakespeare, including *The Secret Diary Of A Call Girl*, *Scar Tissue* and *St Trinians* 2.

Once, when I called in on Colin to record a radio interview, Kirsty, his lovely theatre director wife, was out and he was left in charge of their first child, Edith. She was asleep upstairs and all was well. Colin chose the kitchen to record the interview. While I was setting up, unbeknown to me, he had started the washing machine. It proved great fun and Colin gave a kind of commentary of how it was progressing, during the recording, and even announced the final spin.

I have always followed Colin's career with great interest and just love his company – and the thrill of not quite knowing what's going to happen next.

CHAPTER 57

Judy Gascoyne

WHEN JUDY GASCOYNE came live into my radio show, I introduced her after playing Bob Dylan's *Lay Lady Lay*. It made her quite emotional, as she'd looked after the iconic American singer/songwriter when he stayed at Forelands Farm, Bembridge. This was when he starred in the epic 1969 Wootton Pop Festival.

I'll never forget her opening words. "That's my favourite Bob Dylan record and it brings back so many special memories. His lovely green eyes, his shyness and his charm."

In fact, she was Judy Lewis at the time and almost didn't take up the job of looking after him. Her young people, Kevin and Sue, were huge Dylan fans and talked her into it. In the end, she accepted the challenge with just a little trepidation, which later proved groundless.

The promoters hadn't given Judy much of a food budget to look after a superstar and eight others, including George Harrison. The kitchen facilities were somewhat basic, with just one saucepan and a kettle. None of the Bembridge shops would give her credit and she barely had enough food to go around. For this reason, Dylan was seen in the nearby David's Supermarket, with his own shopping basket, much to the delight of the staff.

Judy told me: "When Bob asked me if George Harrison and his wife could also stay, it meant I had to sleep on the kitchen floor."

When Bob first arrived, much later than anticipated, Judy had arranged sandwiches for his party, which included his wife.

"He darted about like a lynx and seemed a little restless but was so polite. He asked for honey with his breakfast, so I had to dash out and buy some."

Judy loved their supper meals together. Bob insisted she joined them and served the food. There were ten, including her, at the table. She was not fazed at all and would not let George Harrison get away without washing up. He complained that Bob was always excused this chore. She explained he was the star and did not have to do it.

"After supper, when the washing up was done, Bob always sang for me. He would sing any song that I requested. He always told me he'd enjoyed the food and was so much more courteous than any of the others."

Judy's fond memories included watching them playing rather bad tennis, seeing The Band rehearse in the barn and collecting so many star autographs. She also told me she saw no alcohol or drugs during Bob's stay in Bembridge. Judy also found George Harrison to be something of an extrovert. He was very outgoing but with no side to him at all. He would often interview her with many questions. She also admired the real friendship between Bob and George.

"The promoters asked me to prepare for a party after Bob's return from Wootton. They asked if I could organise a large buffet for people like John Lennon and Yoko and numerous other stars. I wanted to go and see Bob perform but was told this was not possible, as I had to get everything ready at Bembridge. I told Bob about this and he said he didn't want a party and that I could come to the concert. I was sat a row or two from John Lennon."

Judy, who later married celebrated poet David Gascoyne, made programmes for the IW Hospital Radio for well over 20 years. She was such a keen member of the Women's Institute and did so much for local charities. Not many people can claim to have had Bob Dylan as their after dinner troubadour.

CHAPTER 58

Snowy White

I FIRST MET Snowy White in 1981. I'd been tipped off by a Weekly Post reader that he'd joined Thin Lizzy. I contacted his father Don, a well known local driving instructor and dance band musician, and he told me that Snowy was soon coming home for a Sunday visit and would be pleased to see me.

Snowy was one of those legendary West Wight rock musicians who began in local bands like Outer Fringe and Perception. He always had a leaning towards playing blues guitar, which led him to eventually front his own blues band. In his early guitar days he used to play at the Towers Holiday Centre, Thorness, where his father played in their dance band.

Before finding fame with Thin Lizzy, and then with his own solo chart success, he'd played guitar for Steve Harley, Al Stewart, Cliff Richard, Joan Armatrading and Linda Lewis. He'd also toured as an augmented musician for Pink Floyd.

He told me back in '81: "With the Floyd, I was an extra musician and I just stood still on stage. Now, as a full member of Thin Lizzy, I'm in the spotlight out front playing solo guitar and having a say in what goes on."

With Lizzy he toured the Far East and Australia and with Phil Lynott out front they were a force to be reckoned with. He also recorded with the band and appeared on two of their albums.

"We all get on so well, which is perhaps surprising. When I first joined I wondered how long it would be before the clouds began to gather. They have never come.

"Basically, I'm not that out-going. Just an old blues guitar player. In fact, I won't worry if it suddenly packs up."

In the end, Snowy did confess to have had enough and left because he was not impressed with the musical direction they were aiming for. He had plans for a possible solo career and was given a deal with Towerbell Records, who backed him to write his own songs. When B*ird Of Paradise* flew into the pop charts and made the Top Ten it had all been worth it. I recorded his appearance on *Top Of The Pops* – and still have it. What a song that was! Several others made the lower reaches of the charts and he was a major pop star for a while. I have a feeling he felt more comfortable when he formed his own Snowy White Blues Band. They made some incredible albums. This has continued for many years and I love one called *Released*, which came out in 2016. It's seldom out of my car.

Snowy appeared live on my radio show several times and he came back home for occasional appearances. There were gigs at Lakeside, Wootton, and Newport's Medina Theatre. The latter was the only time I've ever been disappointed with Snowy White. It was with his own blues band but, for some reason, he decided not to perform his pop hit B*ird Of Paradise*. You could virtually sense all of his audience were waiting for it.

I readily admit to being a fan of Snowy's for many years, both as a guy and as a very accomplished guitar player.

CHAPTER 59

Derek Smith

DURING THE '60s and beyond one of the most famous men on the Island was a guy called Derek Smith, otherwise known as the 'one-arm bandit king.' He was certainly a local boy made good and, quite rightly, was very proud of that fact. I invited him on to my radio show and a few days before, we had a get together at his wonderful house at Kite Hill, Wootton. It was way beyond the means of a dental technician.

Initially, Derek was an apprentice to Cowes dentist Bobby Lowein. Eventually he moved to Richard Collinson's practice, in the town's Bath Road, and it was there that he also moved into slot machines, as a little earner in his spare time. That was certainly a shrewd move – and Derek told me a great story to prove it.

"When I was working at Richard's practice, one of his patients congratulated him on his brand new Jaguar car parked outside. He had to admit it was not his. It belonged to his technician."

Derek's gamble certainly paid off. He very quickly had 600 slot machines around the Island and was certainly coining in the money. His budding empire corresponded with the '60s boom for both music and living standards. It was more exciting than making false teeth.

"In those days there was a lot of profit sharing on many of the machines and it was important to seek out the latest models to achieve the best possible takings," said Derek.

When Derek was not able to drive for a while, he certainly had a huge mountain of a guy as his chauffeur. He could also take care of business, if necessary. Not everyone was thrilled by his success as a businessman.

Derek was never frightened to speak his mind, as Alex Dyke found out on his notorious local radio phone-in.

During his first appearance on my programme he told thousands of listeners: "It's a very funny feeling on the Isle of Wight. Any local lad who's successful on the Island, remains on the Island and refuses to join in with the organised crowd, then becomes a black sheep. The first thing they say about you is that you are a likeable rogue. I have never had any ambition to become a worshipful master."

It was a well known fact that Derek had no time for the Freemasons movement and he criticised them in public for several years.

There was no disputing that Derek Smith was a very canny businessman. In some cases, he was almost ahead of the game. For a while he had local cafes, including two in Ventnor and others in Yarmouth, Newport, Ryde and East Cowes. Then he moved into nightclubs, which included The Gloster, The Birdcage, which became The Gatsby, and Squires.

Derek bought the complete Blue Lagoon complex, in Sandown, and in the bar he gave budding young Island musicians the chance to perform. He was so flattered when he met Mark King, again, after his worldwide success with Level 42. Mark thanked him for his first ever music gigs, at the Blue Lagoon.

A few years later I think Derek missed a business opportunity. On his own admission, in 1977 he was a fat 18 stone businessman, going to seed. In just six weeks he lost over 5 stone. It could have been 'Lose Weight The Derek Smith Way.' I passed him in the street and didn't even recognise him.

After 28 years of non activity, he went back into competitive cycle racing and restricted himself to 700 calories a day. He even completed our 62 mile round the Island race in just 3hrs 42 minutes. As a youngster, he'd clocked 1 hour four minutes and 12 seconds for a 25 mile event, as a Vectis Roads junior.

CHAPTER 60

Brian Morey

IN THE GLORY DAYS of Island League football Brian Morey was one of our greatest entertainers, especially when the red mist set in. His clashes with opponents and match officials are still talked about, especially when old players get together. What some of them don't know is that 'Mad Morey' is now a champion pony breeder, can recite Tennyson poems and has a heart of gold. He scrubs up really well, too.

I was lucky enough to witness the real friendship between Brian and the late Island-based actor, Geoffrey Hughes. They were great pals and enjoyed each others company

so much. Both of them grew up on council estates and were so proud of that fact. At the wake, following Geoff's funeral, Brian met up with Tricia Penrose, who played Gina the barmaid in Heartbeat. When I took her back to the ferry the next morning, she told me she'd never met anyone quite like Brian Morey. I knew what she meant.

I remember being invited to his 70th birthday party at Newport Football Club – although he still tells me I was never actually invited. Halfway through the evening a guy in a huge cloak, a big felt black hat and a scarf, hiding his face, burst into the room carrying a red book. He asked Brian to join him in the middle of the room. Mr Morey looked somewhat bemused but joined the mystery guy, with some trepidation. Apparently, his mother-in-law was among the guests. He had no idea who was in the cloak. Thankfully, he took it so well and we're still great friends.

Brian would make a perfect travel guide for Gunville. He was born there and is still such a fan of the place. He even financed the Gunville signs that you see when entering the village. He was very adamant that it was not Carisbrooke. He's got a fund of funny stories from his early days in the village, involving Eli Coshall and other mates.

During his life, Brian controlled the building of hundreds of local new houses, particularly in Binstead. He was so good at his job and his workers were very loyal. There is so much to like about Brian Morey.

His football stories would fill half of this book. On several occasions he left the game early, on the advice of a man in black. Once he was carried off with his leg broken in two places. He'd tackled an opponent so hard that the crack sounded like a 12 bore rifle shot.

"They took my socks off, got a broom handle and tied it to my leg with the socks. This acted as a splint. They put a coat over me, laid me down on the touchline and carried on playing. It was raining and I had to wait 45 minutes for an ambulance."

Throughout his career he was the guy opponents loved to hate. Luckily, he also had the chance to play with some brilliant local footballers. He did play Hampshire League football for Newport Reserves for a while. Most remember him for his days with Parkhurst Old Boys.

Brian emigrated to Australia for a while and, would you believe, got into trouble with referees. In one game he took on five Greeks in the opposing team and the German referee walked off and left them to it. I did hear a rumour that he had two different names in Australian football. I can guess why! He eventually retired from football to play golf – but got no further than Brown's pitch and putt at Sandown.

That Morey smile is still very captivating and he's as popular as ever.

I was actually there on the day in 2017 that he actually hugged his old sparring partner Oscar Stretch. It was about time – and a moment to savour.

CHAPTER 61

The Cherokees

WITH DUE RESPECT to other Island '60s groups, The Cherokees, with their legendary line-up of Graham Betchley, Brian Sharpe, Crann Davies and Ken Young, were the band everyone talked about and they constantly sold out venues wherever they played. The group, with a completely different personnel, had evolved in the previous decade and thrilled crowds at the Queens Hall, Newport, now the Boots store.

During their illustrious career in local music they were never prone to originality. They were happy to be influenced by the latest craze from Tin Pan Alley or the current record charts. In their early days they were influenced by rock 'n' roll giants like Buddy, Elvis and Cliff.

When the Beatles conquered the world's pop scene the Cherokees joined the charge and were rather clever. They would buy the latest Beatles record on a Saturday morning, learn it, rehearse it and then include it in their ballroom gig the same night.

They were on the same Ryde Pavilion bill as the Rolling Stones in 1964 and it was a memorable day for them. It's rumoured the promoter paid just £150 for Jagger and co. They also supported top acts like Matt Monro, the Animals, Lulu and the Yardbirds, at the Commodore Cinema.

The Cherokees local EP, containing one of their showstoppers, *Anthony Boy*, sold out in quick time. I loaned mine to the daughter of my office boss and never got it back. In more recent years a CD containing their live and studio tracks has been released. Two of their own songs, *Deep Blue Feeling*, which was a single in Sweden, coupled with Brian Sharpe's *I Feel Good*, and a third, *Between The Lines*, proved they were more than a covers band.

They promoted their own shows as the 69 Club, most fondly remembered at the Royal York Hotel, Ryde. They brought in groups like the Moody Blues, T-Rex, Nice, Family, Fairport Convention and original American rock ' n roll star Gene Vincent.

The group almost made the charts in 1970 with their only nationally released single *Candle In The Wind*, recorded as Wilfred, on Parlophone Records. It was produced by Amen Corner's Alan Jones and was augmented by a 30-piece orchestra. They even met an image maker in London, which wasn't their kind of thing.

In reality, they didn't seek fame as pop stars. They had local families and good steady jobs and were happy to remain that way. They were the Island's very own superstars.

When the disco boom arrived they decided to call it a day. They were very much a real live band. I did attend a one-off 1982 reunion gig at the Wishing Well, Pondwell, which quickly became a house full and there was a long queue outside. The police arrived but not because of any trouble. There were so many cars in the area with no parking lights on and they allowed 20 minutes for fans to put that right. I remember Ken Young telling me they had managed to rehearse 43 numbers in just 14 hours.

I interviewed all four members over the years and it was a pleasure to do so. I surprised Brian Sharpe and Graham Betchley on one occasion and it became one of the greatest moments of their lives – and there was not even a mention of their popular musical duo or other pop groups they had played it. They were my *Weekly Post* Sports Personalities of the week. At the time they both played football for Haylands Reserves.

CHAPTER 62

Roy Westmore

WHEN I HAD my 26 year radio chat show I often tried to have two complete opposites in the same programme. It was with eager anticipation that I decided to present our much respected local businessman and councillor Roy Westmore in the same show as Hollywood movie star Britt Ekland. I don't need to tell you which one proved much more friendly.

Roy was old school and a perfect gentleman. When I interviewed him, he'd been living in the same Chillerton house for 71 years and spent 40 years as a local councillor. For most of that time he didn't fly the flag for any particular party. Like many of us, he rued the day party politics took over in local councils. In 1977 he was forced to take a party ticket and, as a conservative, he had many battles with Morris Barton. He did enjoy their arguments and debates. It was a surprise to both of them when they found out they were related.

I could listen to Roy for hours. He had such a memory and was a man for the community. Thankfully, he was awarded an OBE for this work.

Roy could remember the sheep dipping in Chillerton and collecting turnips from the fields. He also had a long way to go to attend school. He lived next door and just jumped over the wall.

His first job was at Rookley Brickworks and then he moved to Morey's in Newport. He could remember going to local forests and seeing the horses towing the timber to their yard.

Many will remember Roy being involved with the Westmore family business at Blackwater. They were building contractors, funeral directors and, latterly, had a garage and petrol pumps. That was a far cry from his schooldays when he bought a one penny (old money) bar of chocolate from a machine on Blackwater Station. In '63 he was on the final train that ran from Blackwater to Merstone and back. On that sad Sunday night, it was standing room only.

HM The Queen with Roy Westmore

When the Queen made a visit to Yarmouth, at the time Lord Louis Mountbatten was made our Governor, Roy, as the chairman of the IW Rural District Council, spent nearly an hour with her in the town. Was it a daunting task?

"It was fine but you had to do everything as you were instructed. I was particularly pleased with the interest the Queen took in meeting the people from the town."

Her Majesty left Yarmouth by hovercraft and it broke down due to a faulty fuel pump. Roy still remembers Lord Louis Mountbatten's comment: "It was just as well it wasn't an aeroplane."

When Roy appeared on my show, Morris Barton asked if I could play the Virginian theme. It worked like a dream. Roy had gone to Virginia on a civic visit to tie in with their Isle of Wight County. The Virginian hierarchy tried to drink Roy under the table, without success. Our man was invincible.

Roy, who was church warden at Gatcombe Church for over 50 years, was highly honoured to be our High Sherriff. During his year in office he had four Royal visits. These were Princess Diana, Princess Anne, the Duchess of York and the Duchess of Kent. They couldn't have met a nicer Islander.

CHAPTER 63

Bruce Sothcott

IN 1936 A YOUNG Bembridge lad of just 16 won the very first *Go As You Please* talent contest at the Commodore, Ryde. The reward for winning, with his song and dance routine, was not a recording contract or the promise of a professional career. It was just £3 but it changed the life of Bruce Sothcott for ever.

After winning that contest his zest for entertaining the public never diminished. When I first met him, in 1977, he'd just completed 22 years at the Whitecliff Bay Holiday Park. He was so popular and campers came back every year just because he was there. In fact, there was only four foot six inches of him but he certainly made an impact and was like a pied piper to the thousands of children who came to the centre. Only very occasionally was he teased about his size – but he could handle all that. Comments like "I should give up smoking mate, it stunts your growth," were like water off a ducks back. He'd heard it all before.

Bruce was one of a famous Bembridge family and he began performing at the local CE School. In the early '30s he did appear in some Cavendish-Morton garden ballet shows, often as a jockey. In 1936 he went to the Portsmouth Hippodrome to audition for the Carroll Levis radio show but was told his act needed to be seen and not heard. Bruce was convinced that if television had been around he would have become famous. It later happened for Charlie Drake.

Bruce eventually became professional and joined the comedy revue Casey's Court, which toured theatres all over Britain. One of his fellow performers in that show was Peter Glaze. Charlie Chaplin had originally worked for this company. The show closed in 1941, due to the war, but that same year he got an eight-week run in Snow White And The Seven Dwarfs.

Back home in Bembridge, he followed his love for big band music by forming the Rhythmics and they set the joint swinging, with him on drums, at places like the St John's Hall, Sandown. Bruce was also in the Freddie James Band who supported famous name bands like Tito Burns, Nat Gonella and Vic Lewis, when they appeared at Island ballrooms.

Bruce joined the Culver Club Trio in 1955. Initially he played in the band and compered their shows but, latterly, he became so popular as an entertainer, particularly with the children.

"I used to tame them very quickly and they seemed to adore me and just followed me around. I loved those days. I also worked with Jack Warner and Leslie Crowther, when they came to Whitecliff."

For several years Bruce was a member of the Bembridge Young Community Club and appeared in their huge hit shows like *Eternal Colonel*, *Moonshine Man* and *Bandida*, written by Keith Newbery and Robin Burnett. For a while, he was also the leader of Bembridge Youth Club.

I still vividly remember the day he appeared live on my radio chat show. He was scared – but not of me or the programme. There was a massive thunder and lightning storm going on and every few minutes he visibly jumped. Of course, his lovely wife, Nancy, took it all in her stride.

Late in his life, I used to go and visit Bruce in a Bembridge care home and, as you would expect, he was the life and soul of the place. His motto always was: "Keep 'em laughing."

CHAPTER 64

Keith Allen

IN 1962 ONE OF THE Island's most talented footballers was Keith Allen, who played locally for Seaview. He was a part of a Nettlestone football dynasty, which contained several of his brothers, who were also such talented players. Portsmouth signed him from Seaview for £50.

George Smith, his Pompey manager, is probably best remembered for his well publicised comment "there is nothing but fish in the sea around Portsmouth." He disbanded the reserve and youth teams and claimed there was no local talent in the area. He never played Keith in their first team and eventually found him a new club. He went to Grimsby Town as a part of the deal that brought Cliff Portwood to Fratton Park.

Many of us knew that Keith was a far better played than George Smith gave him credit for. To prove it, he went on to play well over 300 Football League and cup games for Grimsby, Stockport, Luton Town and Plymouth.

Grimsby was not a dream move and Keith told me why in our first interview.

"I only played about six times. It was not a happy stay and a family bereavement brought me back home. My mother died and I had to come back and look after the family. I asked the Grimsby boss if I could go back just before the end of the season. He told me to go and take my boots with me, as I was not retained for the next season."

Legendary goalkeeper Bert Trautmann got wind of this and sent one of his Stockport backroom staff to the Island for a summer holiday, with the task of signing Keith. It was mission accomplished. He was an instant success and helped them win the Fourth Division championship, scoring 16 goals.

Then Stockport wanted Luton's Derek Kevan and Keith went the other way as part of the transfer. Luton came out with the best of the deal. Keith played over 150 games for them and scored 36 goals.

He became an instant local legend and played alongside Bruce Rioch and Malcolm MacDonald. More recently, he was one of just four Luton stars to be included on a special souvenir mug.

"I met Bruce Rioch a few years ago and he said thanks for making me. That really made me feel good," said Keith, who won another Fourth Division title and a Third Division runners-up medal with the Hatters.

Keith ended his career at Plymouth Argyle, where he enjoyed another memorable stay and, as at Luton, he became a local personality. Sadly, a knee injury forced him to retire.

"I'll never forgive the Plymouth manager, Tony Waiters. He made me play in a reserve game, with my injury, and it just crumpled. That was the end of my career." He actually stayed on in the city to become a salesman, before moving back to Seaview.

During his career he played against glamour clubs like Manchester City and Leeds but never earned more that £40 a week.

When Sean got married I found out his father-in-law, Ian Stonham, was a Luton fanatic and Keith Allen was one of his great heroes. I had an idea - and Keith was up for it. Sean and Susie were married in Faringdon, Oxon, and a few days later they came back to Godshill Methodist Church, where his late mother, Heather, had been a regular worshipper. After the service we had a special tea and I was thrilled to bring in a surprise guest for Ian. They never stopped talking about Luton Town for nearly half an hour. Thanks Keith.

The last time I popped into Keith's for a cup of tea, he had to stop watching Judge Judy. Sorry mate.

CHAPTER 65

Mike Reader

I FIRST GOT TO KNOW Mike Reader when I was a salesman calling on his father's factory in Freshwater. I took to him straight away and quickly became the butt of a few of his jokes, which I thoroughly enjoyed. I'm not so sure I told him that his lovely sister, Pat, was an old school girlfriend of mine, long before she became a pop star for a few years. I've always thought Mike would have liked to have been a rock star – or a Robert Plant tribute act!

We have been friends for many years and when I asked him about an interview for *The Beacon*, he readily agreed and clearly wanted the real truth, with nothing glossed over. It was the amazing story of a family business that once employed over 300 people and, at that time in 2014, had shrunk to around 26. He'd survived it all, had learnt such a lot about life and come out a more contented person, to enjoy his well earned retirement.

Mike's father, Reg, came to the Island for war service and stayed to build his very successful lampshade empire. They supplied Woolworths. Did he ever have plans for Mike to eventually take over? It was never made clear to him but he started on the shop floor and worked his way up.

"I had a lot of advice from my father. Some I acted on and others I discarded. I have always remembered one thing he told me. It was, to be comfortable all your life and not rich for a year."

Sadly, Mike's father died in the early '70s and during his illness he gave a hand-over party to make his son the managing director. It was suddenly make or break for young Mike. Under his astute command, he more than doubled the turnover and obtained 200 new customers. Readers then had four factories on the Island.

"Some people said why didn't I get a Ferrari but I just didn't want one. For many years I had a Mini, took a sensible salary and worked as hard as I could."

It was a stressful time and he jetted all over the world to build up the business and was away for 150 days a year. This meant missing out so much on family life and led to the breakdown of his marriage, which saddened him.

When a large customer came out of lighting there were redundancies, which nearly broke his heart. He had to rebuild the business.

"I was full of anger inside but I had the attitude that nothing was going to stop me. I was definitely in the fast lane. I also had a major drink problem which didn't help.

"In 1989 an incident happened that changed my life. It was like a car crash type of moment. It brought me to my senses and I have not had a drink for over 25 years."

The company expanded and in the mid '90s they were turning over £28 million a year and had both commercial and financial directors and other high grade staff. Suddenly, it became beyond a family business and he could have been voted out by other directors. For him, Readers had just got too big.

There was a real disaster when a principal customer changed their rules and a lot more money was needed. It meant the company virtually closed down, with major redundancies, and Mike had a nervous breakdown.

"I had such a super staff and I felt I had let them down. Amazingly, most of them felt sorry for me," reflected Mike.

There is a happy ending. Readers was saved and is now run by his family and is a much smaller concern.

Back in their high flying days, Christine Cutler joined Readers from B&Q. That was an inspired choice and she is now Mike's wife – and they are so good for each other.

CHAPTER 66

Jillie Wheeler

WHEN I FIRST MET the Island's amazing fundraiser Jillie Wheeler, she and her husband, Frank, were providing the summer entertainment at Sandown's Sandringham Hotel. The residents loved them and so did a few locals, who managed to slip in. Jillie sang and also recited her wonderful monologues. Frank, a great musician, played piano and was a very able light comedian. Not surprisingly, when his wife was around, he didn't get the chance to say very much.

That was in 1976 and by then they had build up quite a reputation as The Wheelers, having been on Radio 2 shows and numerous cruises, for which they were always so much in demand. They had also enjoyed a summer season at Sandown Pavilion.

Back in the '60s, Jillie had been a make-up artist and she worked backstage at the 1963 *Royal Variety Show*. During her time at ATV she made up stars like Morecambe and Wise and Charlie Drake. On *Emergency Ward* 10 most of the wounds and scars were her handy work.

Jillie found more than she bargained for when she joined P&O as a cruise hostess. She ended up marrying the bandleader and they became a double act, on and off stage. On one occasion, when we met, Frank did actually have a few words to say. I'm sure he was joking!

"That was probably the biggest mistake of my life. We met in the middle of the Indian Ocean and I really should have pushed her overboard there and then."

Jillie did have a reply: "Frank always teased me and said that I only married him because I wanted a tame piano player."

During her showbiz career Jillie worked with names like Frankie Howerd, Leslie Crowther, Julie Rogers, Jack Douglas and Trevor Bannister.

Her *Gardener's Lament* monologue proved so popular and was featured on a tea towel, which the holidaymakers loved. I'll never forget the time her and Frank came live on to my Sunday lunchtime chat show. Suddenly, a few minutes before Jillie was due to recite her most famous monologue, she left the studio. When she returned she was dressed as a gardener, to get into character. Frank said very little, other than: "Jillie this is radio and not television." It worked, anyway.

With the help of her German Shepherd dogs, particularly Cassie, Jillie has raised over £100,000 for worthwhile charities in past years. The OBE she was awarded was so well deserved. She has written several books to aid charities.

Despite her hearing problems, she has continued to enjoy life. I loved seeing her comedy routines with Danny Lamb, at the Bembridge Village Hall. They were so clever and Jillie could not hear many of his lines, due to her deafness, but you would have never known. Once a performer, always a performer.

The story of Jillie and an undertaker is still my favourite – and it's true. After her beloved Frank died, she was taken to the Bembridge Lane End Cemetery by local undertaker Terry Weaver, to see where his plot was going to be. I'll let her finish the story.

"I held Terry's arm and he took me to the proposed place. I was not happy and told him it was too near the road and Frank hated the noise of traffic. It was also in the shade and I wanted him more in the sun. I saw a cherry tree much further away and told him that was the spot Frank would like – and I got it."

It's never been easy to say no to Jillie Wheeler. She's a people person and so many have benefitted from her tireless efforts

CHAPTER 67

Clive Green

WHEN I BEGAN writing my *Stage Talk* column for the *Weekly Post* in 1975, I met a guy called Clive Green, who ran all the entertainment at the Ponda Rosa roadhouse at Ashey. It led to my early interviews with Roy Castle, Mike and Bernie Winters, Jim Davidson, Acker Bilk and Lonnie Donegan, to name just a few. It also led to Barry Winship throwing knives at me on stage. I'm certain Clive set that one up.

The Ponda was special and their Saturday night dinner dances sold out every week. Their star cabaret nights attracted locals from all over the Island. I'll never forget the night the Wurzels first came back to the Ponda, without their leader, Adge Cutler, who had tragically died in a car crash. For Pete Budd, Tommy Banner and Tony Baylis it was a night to remember. Their *Combine Harvester* record was top of the charts and, somehow, over 500 crammed into the venue. This was long before health and safety started to spoil everyone's fun.

I can vividly remember the Mike and Bernie Winters night when Clive had real sound problems and he even had to go on stage to try and sort it out. In a way, it made the night even more enjoyable. They gave Clive a verbal roasting, which brought the house down. Being such a sport, he took it all so well. Forty years later I'm still writing about it. It was a magical night.

Clive did have a few problems, particularly after he'd left Lonnie Donegan at the end of Ryde Pier, to catch the last ferry back to the mainland. He was home and in bed when Lonnie rang to say the fog had come down and the ferry was cancelled. The skiffle king was not amused but Clive found him an hotel.

The Ponda also made headlines all around the world for their notorious hen nights. The ladies loved the male strippers and really let their hair down. The most popular were The Pink Panther, The Viking and King Dick.

It wasn't until after the family had sold the Ponda Rosa that I discovered the real Clive Green story. No wonder he took the Mike and Bernie night in his stride. Previously, he'd been a captain in the Royal Army Ordnance Corps and commanded a bomb disposal unit.

In 1967, he'd been summoned to mid-Wales to inspect a suspected terrorist device, containing a clock and 40 sticks of gelignite. It trailed into the water under a viaduct, on a route that carried most of Birmingham's water. Two officers should have gone but as it was a Sunday, and actually his 25th birthday, he had to go on his own. The police were agitated, so he had to go solo. He did manage to enlist a police inspector, who took cover behind a nearby tree, to make a note of what he was doing, in case of an accident. Clive re-lived it again for me.

"The terminals were actually touching so, in theory, it should have gone off. Eventually, I pulled up a tyre inner tube with the 40 explosives in it. I then had to find a field to explode 38 of the sticks. The other two went to the police for checking."

It was all in a day's work for Clive and he went off to enjoy a cup of tea and didn't even let his family know. Back in the office the next morning he was besieged by national newspapers and TV cameras. It was a bomb hero storyline.

"When my mother found out what I'd actually done in Wales, I had a real telling off," recalled Clive.

CHAPTER 68

Jack Plucknett

IN 1934 JACK PLUCKNETT'S father told him he was going to retire and sell the milking herd at Newport's Whitepit Dairy. Jack was surprised but there was more bad news to follow. Dad did not even want him to take over the family business, started in 1886. He was told to go and get a trade. That was the sole reason he became a hairdresser. I caught up with him 71 years later and he was still cutting hair.

If farming was tough, being a trainee hairdresser had to be even more of a vocation. At Alfred Riley's, in Nodehill, Jack worked weekdays from 7-30am, with early closing on Thursdays at 1pm. On Saturday nights he worked until at least 9pm. That was Newport's busiest night of the week, as people flocked in from country areas.

That was not all. On four mornings a week, at 6am, he cycled to the Newport Workhouse and Infirmary to shave and cut hair in the old men's quarters and the mental wards. At the latter, one patient was suddenly prone to put his head between his legs. Jack had to be alert with a cut throat razor in his hand. Then he cycled off to work. On

Sunday mornings he went back to the Infirmary to cut the hair of bedridden patients. All for 3/6d a week, that's about 18p in today's money.

Jack was a real snazzy dresser and in his younger days he resembled screen idol Richard Todd. During his early days of hairdressing, he shaved and cut the hair of John Mills, who married a local girl, and famous author JB Priestley, who lived at Brook.

Four years after leaving the farm, he bought a packet of 20 cigarettes from Tomlinson's the tobacconist's and it changed his life for ever. They cost him just 5p, in today's money. Cheekily, on his way out, he made a date with the shop manageress, Rita Day. They went to the Odeon to watch a Sabu movie. They left him with his elephant, and spent a lifetime together. They were so well suited and shared their passion for gardening, which was Rita's domain, and classical music.

In the '50s, Jack was diagnosed with TB and spent two years at the Havenstreet Sanatorium, before returning to work in Ryde. Eventually, he joined Porter's in Newport's Pyle Street. In 2005, when I last interviewed Jack, that old shop was something different.

"The old Porter's premises is now called a private shop and you can't see in the windows. I don't know what that's all about," suggested Jack. He didn't sound that convincing.

In 1962 when Nodehill barber Fred Barnes passed away, his wife offered Jack the chance to take it over. It was a shrewd move and he stayed there until 1998. His daughter, Lynne, managed the upstairs ladies salon.

On one occasion, charismatic local musician John Wroath asked for his head to be shaved and requested 15 tram lines on one side. Jack duly obliged but the next morning, John's father, a notable local judge, went in to complain. I'm not sure if our music hero had to wear his dad's wig!

Jack was 86 when I did his *County Press* article and he was still cutting hair for friends and family. Sadly, he took one look at me and said it was really too late – although I did assure him I once had a huge head of hair.

As I left he whispered: "Do you want anything for the weekend?" Force of habit, I suppose!

CHAPTER 69

Steve Ross

ALTHOUGH HE ENDED UP as Baron Ross of Newport, in the House of Lords, following his term as the Island's MP from 1974 until 1987, to thousands of Islanders he was still that very likeable man, Steve Ross. He was also known for playing cricket for Westover and being a local auctioneer. I can't think of a more popular Island MP.

In 1974, a year after I'd moved from East Cowes to Godshill, I had a knock on my door and it was the Island's Liberal candidate Steve Ross. I'd played cricket against him and was just surprised to see him on a door knocking campaign in the village. I promised him my vote – but I never mentioned this to my father, who was a red hot Labour supporter. I was among thousands who decided to do the same thing and it caused a sensation when he beat Mark Woodnutt.

In 1992 I decided to invite Steve to make a live Sunday lunchtime appearance on my radio show. I wanted the real story of that sensational 1974 victory, which came after two unsuccessful previous attempts.

"As the leader of the IW Council I was at a meeting and someone suggested that they would probably not see me for a week or two, as Ted Heath had called an election. This was the first I knew about it. I only had three weeks."

He went to the drab Liberal office in Newport's Lower St James Street, cleaned it up and waited for the phone to ring. The only person to call was a local press reporter, who wanted to know when his adoption meeting was, as the other two major parties had announced theirs.

"I said to my wife, it looks like you and me and that greasy hired Land Rover again. She was not keen and I decided to wait and see if I had a call from a Liberal supporter. If no-one phoned, I wouldn't stand.

"Around 8-30pm, Tony Brindle, from the Ryde hovercraft service, who I didn't know very well, offered to help. That made me decide to go for it, although I wasn't really confident of any success."

When people continually climbed up two flights of stairs at the Newport office, just to pick up stickers, he was rather shocked. Then on a Saturday morning when a colleague went to the Lugley Street car park, every other car took a sticker. Could the impossible happen?

"My wife asked, what happens if you win? I told her not to be stupid. I'd hate it and would have to get Johnny out of the army and deal with housing problems and all things like that."

Steve made it and became a very popular MP. He had so many letters and requests. Reggie Kray asked him for a prison visit, a West Ham supporter even asked him to get two Cup Final tickets, which he got, and he managed to negotiate to get an Island lady out of a Marrakech jail.

One foggy night in Portsmouth his powers were really put to the test. Over 100 of his constituents were stranded, as the last Fishbourne car ferry was full. It was the old open deck ship. The Ryde Pier service had been cancelled.

He went on board and pleaded with the skipper, who said he would lose his licence if he took more people on board.

"I told him I would go to the Old Bailey, if necessary. These people had to get back to the Island. I was so relieved when I finally managed to persuade him and was able to walk down the ramp and call them all on board."

It's such an accolade to Steve that people still fondly talk about him 25 years after his death.

CHAPTER 70

Jonathan Griffiths

WHAT A STORY Jonathan Griffiths had! The young Islander began as a footballer for Newport Youth, under manager Dale Young, and eventually played both rugby and rugby league for Wales. Amazingly, Sandown High teacher Trevor Wray tempted him into playing rugby and he made his Hurricanes first team debut at the age of 14. Three of his teachers were in that team, Trevor, Gus Baker and John Endacott.

Many years ago we had a family holiday in Wales and after the children had gone to bed in our Cardiff hotel, Heather and I went down into the lounge bar with our books. Journalists always have one ear on any conversations and I was just thrilled to sit there eavesdropping on a few Welsh rugby fanatics, who were actually talking about Jonathan Griffiths. The very next day I was going to Swansea to interview him for the *Weekly Post*.

His Sandown Hurricanes first game was against the London Midland Bank and he had three minders in that fifteen, who kept an eye on any over-welcoming opponents.

In 1998, looking back, he told me: "I was a 14-year old playing in senior rugby. Something could easily have gone wrong. It wouldn't happen today."

Once in a local derby with the Isle of Wight Rugby Club, the whole opposing pack trod all over him. Little did they know they were educating a future Wales scrum half into the more seedier side of the game. He even admitted, he was close to tears on that occasion. It was nothing like that a few years down the line when he helped Llanelli beat Cardiff in a Welsh Cup Final, in front of 40,000 in the National Stadium.

Jonathan, who was actually born in Wales, eventually moved back home from the Island and was forced to play junior rugby to earn a sort of pedigree, a major factor on moving upwards in Welsh rugby. He was spotted by Llanelli and never looked back.

Our ex-Hurricane was chosen for the Welsh 1988 World Cup squad but broke a collarbone and his dreams of a cap went on hold. That finally happened in New Zealand, against the world champions.

"We had a young side that day against the All Blacks and it was so tough but great experience. Luckily, my father (Ron Griffiths the former Shanklin cricketer) was able to fly out and see me win my first cap."

He went on to win several more caps and was on the bench 30 times. In a Five Nations, he was in top form against Scotland and looked a cert to become a regular, until an injury forced him out for a while. It was such a tough task to get back, with Robert Jones in such great form.

"It wasn't easy because Robert's father-in-law was the chairman of the selectors," rued Jonathan. Eventually, he'd had enough of the old pals act and was tempted into going professional with St Helens (no not Goose Island), the famous rugby league club. He gave up his job as a fireman.

Jonathan Davies had started the Welsh exodus to rugby league and our ex-Sandown High boy followed suit. When he managed to score the two tries that took St Helens to a Wembley final, he was carried off the field to celebrate, in front of 32,000. He was also capped for the Wales national rugby league team and the Great Britain side.

A past question on A *Question Of Sport* was to name the person who had represented Wales at three different sports. Yes it was Jonathan – as he also played cricket for Wales. He once hit 177 for his country. Adrian, his brother, also played cricket for Wales.

CHAPTER 71

Vic Farrow

I'LL NEVER FORGET one particular Sunday lunchtime in late 1993. As I left the radio station a guy was waiting for me in reception. He introduced himself as Vic Farrow. Then he told me he liked my show and would I be interested in interviewing a friend of his? When he told me it was Cliff Richard, I sensed a station wind-up. He looked really genuine and showed me some photographs of him and Cliff. I was not convinced but he asked if I could be at home on Thursday at 1pm, as Cliff's manager would ring me.

Cliff Richard with Vic Farrow

I rushed home at just before the arranged time and within a few minutes the phone rang. I answered and a voice said: "Is that John Hannam? This is Bill Latham, Cliff Richard's manager. So you would like to come up and see us."

I was almost speechless. He was one of the top five people I longed to interview. We fixed a date for about six weeks later. I suddenly could even remember where I had first heard Cliff Richard's *Move It* record. I was in Murdoch's music shop in Newport and a Cowes guy called Alan Bowen came in and asked to hear the record. Everyone just stood and listened to the amazing sound coming from the record booth. I think we all bought it.

On the day of the interview, Vic collected me from my Godshill home and drove me to Cliff's Surrey offices, where he had a staff of around 30. The office girls even gave me lunch. Vic was a trustee of Cliff's Pro/Celebrity Tennis Tournament.

I've treasured our friendship over the years and still vividly remember regular visits to his Screen Deluxe cinema in Lake. It was such a wonderful taste of real cinema, as we once knew it. Vic was more interested in his customers enjoying the movie than filling them up with overpriced popcorn and drinks. He came on my radio show on the fifth anniversary of his 150-seat cinema. Their first-ever movie had been *Indiana Jones And The Last Crusade*. Up until then, his most successful movie had been *Aladdin*. Sadly, in the end, the arrival of the Newport's huge multiplex cinema made it hard to compete with.

In more recent years, Vic has become known for his invaluable work to really put Shanklin Theatre back on the map. His ingenuity has brought several huge names to the theatre.

Over the years Vic has arranged so many interviews for me and I have been so grateful. No artist has ever had a bad word to say about him. Many have gone out of their way to say how well he's looked after them. However, Vic is no easy ride. Some ridiculous riders from artists or their management do not always get the Farrow approval.

Vic has collected autographs all his life and these include Buddy Holly, Bob Hope and Sean Connery. I love his Frank Sinatra story, which he revealed on-air.

"I knew a doorman at London's Savoy Hotel. When Sinatra was appearing in London concerts, I was told he often goes out of the side door. There were just three of four of us stood there and suddenly six bodyguards came out with radios and two huge cars turned up. We were told he sometimes signed autographs. Frank came out, got into his car, nodded to his bodyguard and then he called us over one at a time. I was so lucky."

Vic was also a great fan of Jack Palance and when he politely asked him for an autograph, in a London street, the Hollywood legend asked him, in his world famous movie drawl, "what's you name?" It was a scary moment but had a happy ending and he signed the book 'To Victor.'

CHAPTER 72

Tony Best & Mike Nobbs

BESTY AND NOBBY were one of the best double acts on the Island, due to their antics on and off football and cricket pitches. Many thought they hated each other. Far from it. They were simply great pals. Not surprisingly, Tony Best had a lot more to say than Mike Nobbs. In 1988 I must have had a blind spot. I invited them to be the Sports Personality Christmas guests in my *Weekly Post* column.

There was a surprise right at the start – which shook both Mike and myself. We were almost lost for words – and it was all down to Tony.

"Nobby, you have got to do some talking in this Christmas special," suggested Besty.

That promised a dramatic change in their long friendship, which had begun when they were ten-year olds. Would it last? There is no need to answer that.

What were they like as schoolboys when they played in the same Subbuteo League team?

"Nobby used to cheat terribly. He pushed the players instead of flicking them," revealed Tony." His mate replied: "Of course I didn't. How can you sit there and say such a thing." Nobby didn't remember that Tony was once sent out of a house for cheating. Perhaps it was just as well.

Tony Best and Mike Nobbs

Later they played in the same Whitecroft cricket team – and poor Nobby took more than his share of stick. When Besty was skipper, he had his best pal chasing the ball all around the field – and he showed him no mercy.

"The problem with Mike is he just gets under one of the trees near the boundary and loses himself. No wonder we moan when the ball goes sailing past him."

Nobby did have an ace in the pack. Once he actually won the club's bowling trophy. Would his team mate be generous in his praise?

"Of course that was the season they lost the scorebook – and it's never been found." The trophy winner suggested it had been found.

Apparently, just the once, in a game on the mainland, Tony actually said "well bowled Nobby."

In a match against BHC, Nobby scored 36 runs, all in the same innings and on a very tricky pitch. He claimed it was worth a lot more.

"How many did you get in that game Besty?" asked Nobby. There was a rather modest reply. "I got a duck, which was a little unfortunate."

When the subject of football came up, Mike was keen to point out he supported Newport and went to the whole match, unlike a friend of his who went in at half-time because it was free. Not Tony Best, surely!

On a Saturday night in 1990 I invited them both into my live radio chat show. It was going to be a great occasion, as it was planned for Edwin Starr to join us, as he was appearing at Bogeys later that night. Mike and Tony were the warm-up act. When Edwin failed to turn up, they had the whole hour to themselves. They did a brilliant job. We also talked about their endless work for local charities.

Another gem of a moment came when the legendary George Best appeared on my chat show, which had been moved to a Sunday lunchtime. Tony turned up outside the studio for a picture with the superstar but time was tight. I had to run George and Rodney Marsh back to the Red Jet and suggested Tony followed us. There was a happy ending and he got his picture with his more famous namesake. So it was George Best of Manchester United fame and Tony Best from Parkhurst Reserves.

Sadly George, Tony and Mike all died much too young.

CHAPTER 73

Bill Padley

I FIRST MET BILL PADLEY in late February 1983. At that time, be was boldly taking on Terry Wogan, Mike Read and the new breakfast television shows. I was up at 5-30am to head to the Portsmouth studios of Radio Victory, where Bill hosted their very popular breakfast show. Neither of us could have imagined that a few years later he would work for Radio Clyde, the huge Scottish station, win an Ivor Novello Award, produce Julia Fordham's first single and album and be involved with four number one chart hits. In amongst those successes, in 1990, he also became the most popular presenter on the newly launched Isle of Wight Radio.

Bill, who grew up on the Island, was a fan of Radio Victory from the moment they came on air. His love of radio led him to build his own studio in Sandown, where his parents owned a shop. He knew what he wanted, having broadcast at Sandown High, and he pestered Radio Victory so much they eventually gave him a job.

I remember getting a phone call from Bill asking if he could bring a local singer over to the Vine Inn, at St Helens. The lady in question, who lived on Hayling Island, worked in the offices of Radio Victory. I gave this lady a write-up in the *Weekly Post*. Her name was Jules. Several years later I met her again on several occasions. She was then world famous singer Julia Fordham. Guess who produced her first hit single and album?

Bill loved working at Isle of Wight Radio and even produced my show for a while. He gave me great encouragement and was genuinely interested in my career – and this has continued ever since. His fame was spreading and he eventually moved to London to become one of the founders of the UK's biggest radio production company.

His talents as a songwriter and record producer led him to huge success and an involvement with four number one hit singles. It was nice to note that he also kept in touch with his old pals, yours truly included.

One of his greatest moments was receiving an Ivor Novello Award for co-writing the year's biggest hit single, Shayne Ward's *That's My Goal*. This beat Madonna's record for being the biggest download in history and it also sold over a million records. Such was his fame, within the industry, when Gary Barlow heard that Bill had won it, he asked to present it.

Bill had mega hits with Holly Valance and Atomic Kitten and his songs, many written with Jemm Godfrey, were also recorded by Ronan Keating and Blue. He had his own studio, within his flat, in West Hampstead. Top artists loved the informality of it and others who recorded there included Lulu.

My favourite Bill Padley story involves Ronan Keating. Ronan was recording at Bill's flat but they had to stop because builders in the flat above were making too much noise.

"I suggested to Ronan that it might be better if he went up to complain. Imagine the builders surprise when he knocked the door to ask if they could keep the noise down a wee bit. It suddenly went quiet and we recorded the track," said Bill.

I recorded an interview with Bill at his home and, of course, he was a perfect host. He also helped me out on another occasion – and was delighted to do so. I had an interview in West Hampstead but didn't have a venue to record it. A quick phone call to Bill Padley and my problem was solved. He also loved meeting my surprise guest – Burt Kwouk. It was coffee and biscuits with Cato and Bill.

CHAPTER 74

Alby Payne

BACK IN 2000, Carisbrooke's Alby Payne, who ran the Castle View Cafe with his lovely wife Jean, invited me to an early morning breakfast. Actually, it was for an article I was writing for the *County Press*. I decided to go without my granola cereal and grapefruit juice, just in case. When the CP photographer turned up they produced the biggest breakfast I had ever seen in my life. It scared the life out of me – and I just wasn't hungry anymore. It would have lasted me about three days. Unlike me, some of their customers were always banging on their door at the crack of dawn for an Alby and Jean breakfast. According to the proprietor, they were calorie free!

Alby, one of life's natural entertainers, was an original London teddy boy whose life was suddenly inspired by Elvis Presley. Victor Silvester at the Hammersmith Palais never seemed quite the same again. Alby actually met Jean, then a 16-year old teddy girl, in a ballroom. Initially, her dad was not too happy with her latest flame. In the end, he mellowed and they became great pals.

Many of Alby's mates got high powered jobs. He didn't need to wear a posh suit or a starched shirt. He would have been overdressed for a market trader.

"I could sell anything but you always worried about having your collar felt. I wasn't legitimate then but I am today. It was always easy to say you bought it from a guy in a pub. Now they say it came from a guy at a car boot sale," said Alby, back in 2000. I guess it would now be from a guy on eBay.

When they came to the Island in 1985, to look for a business, they found one in Carisbrooke. It was The Country Basket. Alby, then 24 stone, couldn't cope with all the health foods the previous owners had left behind – they didn't go with chips.

He could just about boil water when they opened the cafe. Business was so slow he used to plead with old ladies just to come in the place and buy something, or he would have to close down. Schoolchildren came in for a plate of chips and 15 forks or a can of coke and eight straws. Thankfully, in the end the business boomed.

Always keen to help charities and local groups, Alby raised thousands of pounds for the Newport Boxing Club. When the late Island MP Steve Ross talked him into a sponsored slim, to aid the club, he joined several others who were equally well proportioned.

"I'd never seen so many fat people in my life. At that time, I was over 24 stone. They used the bakery scales to weigh us in and I put on a large overcoat and filled my pockets with weights and bricks. At the final weigh-in, without my overcoat, I'd lost the most. It was about two stone but everyone said I looked the same. They even doubled my sponsor money and it all went to a good cause," revealed Alby.

He has only ever been lost for words once – and that was by Royal Appointment. They were invited to Buckingham Palace for a garden party, for all their work for charity.

"I turned around and walked straight into Prince Philip. He asked me where I came from and I mumbled the Isle of Wight. Then he mentioned Cowes Week. I wasn't quite sure what I said but I think I invited him to our cafe."

CHAPTER 75

Alan & Maureen Osborne

SOME OF US can remember when loyalty was one of the most important things in life. Binfield's Alan and Maureen Osborne are perfect examples. Oz has been involved with the same Island football club for 70 years and was employed by the SEB for 31 years. Maureen has been a member of the IW Keep Fit Association for 38 years and she's worked in Farnsworth's, the Newport newsagents, for over 30 years. They only met through a freezer breakdown. When I interviewed them together, in 2015, they'd been married for 35 years.

I'd interviewed Oz back in 1988 and went to see him again for an article in *The Beacon*. Over a welcoming cup of coffee, I decided I couldn't really do one without the other. So they became the first double act to appear in my monthly column in *The Beacon*.

In January 2017, I decided to go and watch Whitecroft Barton play in a Hampshire Intermediate Cup game. It was a cold day and some spectators, years younger than Oz, sat in the warmth of the clubhouse. That didn't suit him and he was stood on the touchline, as exuberant as ever.

Maureen still manages to keep up with modern cash tills and Fridays in Farnsworth's wouldn't be the same without her.

Oz joined Barton Sports Football Club in 1948 and has never left. He's been everything. A player, committee man, secretary, president, linesman, odd job man and even now gets up a ladder at the clubhouse, until Maureen reads this.

When he worked for SEB, Oz wired up over half the houses on Pan Estate. Then he became one of their first refrigeration engineers. A particular call out changed their lives. More of that later.

When Maureen took a job at Newport's Jubilee Nurseries, Sheila Ball introduced her to the IW Keep Fit Association and she's still going up to three times a week.

"When I first went we did it all in bare feet but times have changed. I think being with this group has given me a wellbeing and the camaraderie is so wonderful. On three occasions, I've even appeared at the Royal Albert Hall."

Oz will never forget that call out to Jubilee Nurseries: "I had to go back a second time for a minor fault. Sheila, the owner, was so pleased to see me and she gave me a quick welcoming cuddle. An assistant called Maureen shouted out, in fun, 'don't I get one, too!' Little did I know what was ahead."

They found out they both had personal problems, at that time, and thought it might be nice to go out together and talk about them. Then came that first date. He arranged to take her for a drink to the Sun Inn, at Calbourne. A last minute phone call from Oz was not of the romantic nature. Would she mind going to East Cowes, instead? He'd been called out to an emergency at Frank James Hospital.

It all ended well. On April Fool's Day, in 1980, they were both divorced and six days later they got married. It was a quiet ceremony, with just two witnesses.

I'm now thinking of writing a Mills and Boon story. True love created by a faulty freezer! Millions of ladies would love to read it. I could add a touch of poetic licence and invent a little bit of extra electricity between them. It would certainly add a certain spark to the story!

CHAPTER 76

Richard Studt

IN 1981 I MADE A determined effort to finally catch up with a local guy called Richard Studt, who was doing so well as a classical musician. His parents owned a cafe and amusement arcade on Ventnor seafront. I was keen to give him some well deserved local recognition and write the first-ever local article on his career. I was not disappointed.

Apparently, he'd been ridiculed as a young Ventnor schoolboy. When he was seen carrying his violin case, followed by a tiny dog, he was jeered and teased by the local lads. Being in short trousers, he was so embarrassed. But he's certainly enjoyed the last laugh.

By the time we first met up, he'd led the London Symphony Orchestra, had been seen on television with Andre Previn, spent five years in the London Mozart Players and led his own trio, the Tate Music Group, at London's Festival Hall.

Then I was completely stunned by his work as a session musician. He'd been on records with the Beatles and Rolling Stones, toured with Roy Orbison and Mike Oldfield and had played on movie soundtracks for *Star Wars* and *Superman*. He described these as: "Bank manager time."

It was a doting Scottish grandmother who had the idea for him to learn the violin, at infant school.

"The older generation could always see a musical ability in youngsters and nurture it. Before long, they had you at Ryde Town Hall, winning a prize in the local music festival," said Richard, who finally ended up at London's Royal Academy Of Music. This was such a relief after an horrendous audition for the National Youth Orchestra.

At the Royal Academy he came into contact with Manoug Parikian, an established soloist, and was one of only four students out of 900, who were lucky enough to study with him.

Richard went on to work with and conduct huge orchestras, including the Bournemouth Symphony, the Philharmonia Orchestra, the Royal Liverpool Philharmonic and the BBC Welsh Orchestra – and others all around the world. In past years he's also appeared many times in Island concerts

Richard also told me of his love for pop music, having been brought up in the Beatles era. He admitted to being jealous at some of the money pop stars earned and a little concerned at how quickly a lot of pop music was forgotten. He came on my radio show several times but could never remember the records of the Beatles and Stones he'd played on.

When he's back on the Island, Richard always visits Whitwell Garage. I met him on their forecourt one day and he turned down my interview request and said I aught to interview his daughter, singer/songwriter Amy Studt, instead. I did just that and have become a great admirer of her work. I've got all her albums and love her brilliant songs like *Misfit*, *Under The Thumb*, *Ladder In My Tights* and, in particular, *Happy Now*, which should be a real standard for years to come. They're certainly a long was from Mozart and the Tate Music Group.

CHAPTER 77

Andrew Taggart

LONG BEFORE Andrew Taggart opened his Round House Tea Room, at Fairlee, he'd never settled anywhere for too long. By then, his life had taken him from his birthplace in Ireland to South Africa, Lancashire, Yorkshire, Hereford, Cyprus, Sussex, Gatwick Airport, Darlington and the Isle of Wight. Some may even remember him as a local Lyons Cakes salesman. To many of us, for 18 years, he was such a popular front man at his local tea room. Customers loved him. He was clearly a ladies man but the guys enjoyed his sense of humour and the fact he was quite harmless.

Seldom seen, but definitely the wind beneath his wings, was his wife Pam. She worked so hard, a fact much appreciated by Andy. If he spent too long chatting up customers, a bell would ring from the kitchen – and did he move!

Andy's father was in the RAF, which meant the family were always on the move. Living in South Africa was a great experience for young Andy. He followed dad into the RAF and stayed for around 11 years. He worked in catering which set him up for life.

He actually met Pam Blackman, whose parents ran North Fairlee Farm, when he was serving in the RAF and, initially, his advances fell on stony ground. In fact, she didn't really want anything to do with him. Things did improve and eventually they got married, in Newport.

After his RAF days, they had restaurants in Sussex and Yorkshire. Later, for several years, he was the catering manager at Gatwick Airport. They sometimes had 10,000 customers in 24 hours. It was nothing to have 400 waiting for breakfasts.

Andy and Pam were looking for a house on the Island and found the Round House was up for sale. They both saw the potential for a tea room and tea garden and it proved such an astute move.

"Thankfully, our tea room became rather special for a lot of local people and we made so many friends. We had such a lot of fun and only gave up because it got too much for us," said Andy.

There were many memories to cherish. Matt and Cat came in for a cream tea and gave them a rave review on their eating out website, read by thousands of people. A few famous guests popped in, including Jimmy Cricket and England footballer Terry Paine. He also appeared three times on my radio show.

Andy was the butt of many jokes – and he loved it. He rang me one day to tell me it was raining frogs at the Round House. I sensed a wind-up but quickly headed for the tea room. I couldn't believe it. There were tiny frogs everywhere - and they'd come from the skies. So, it wasn't a croke!

One day, I had a real shock, whilst walking in Newport High Street. I saw Andy's face on the side of a bus. It was quite scary. Local rumours suggested that, with his face, it should have been on the back of a bus. I'm saying nothing. He does look good for his age – but I wouldn't tell him that.

According to my hairdresser, one day he went into a car wash near his tea room and left his boot open. The brush rollers made the most of it.

On a serious personal note, I would like to thank Andy and Pam for all their kindness, following the death of my wife. Thanks to them, I was able to arrange some charity events at the Round House in aid of the St Mary's Applegate Breast Care Nurses. We raised a few hundred pounds from those functions.

CHAPTER 78

Michael Greenwood

WHEN I PLAYED CRICKET with Michael Greenwood, neither of us could have dreamed what the future had in store for us. He never expected to be literally inches away from huge orang-utans in a Borneo rain forest and I could never have imagined meeting Charlton Heston, John Mills and Richard Todd. For a couple of nippers from East Cowes, we've done ok.

Long before he went into the real jungle, not the TV version, Mike was such a popular Island teacher. There was a group of his former pupils who became known as 'Greenwood's Girls'. They went out for meals together and, on one occasion, 'Sir' found out and surprised them by turning up to join them.

For 32 years he was a teacher at Carisbrooke High. In a way, he went back. He'd attended as a pupil, when it had been the grammar school. It was certainly not his first job but it was his last – and he loved every minute.

He told me in 2015, when we met for an interview: "In those 32 years at Carisbrooke, I only had three days off. When I was a year head I got there at 7am and they had to throw me out around 6pm. I had such an affinity with the place and whilst I was there, I had no abuse from the children at all."

Would he wanted to have gone back, at that stage? "I would not want to teach now and I despair when I read in the press what is happening to education here on the Island. They'd call me a dinosaur now. I've always felt children need boundaries and to know how far they can go or can't go. As a teacher, you are not there as their best mate. I always had all their interests at heart and would do anything for them, but, there was always a line that didn't get crossed."

Originally, Mike wanted to be a graphic designer and studied at Portsmouth Art College. He then moved to London but two years in the big city was more than enough and he headed back home to sort out his life. Before his four-year degree course to become a teacher, he carried meat carcasses in Cowes and sold Mr Whippy ice cream from a van.

As a summer job, during his teacher training, he worked on a Weymouth cross channel ferry. At the end of the season he had two free passes and went to Jersey Zoo. He loved the orang-utans and had a dream to see them in the wild – and he did just that.

The most scary moment he had in that Borneo jungle came when the newly crowned alpha male, Tom, who had broken his rivals arms during the battle for supremacy, suddenly came out of the jungle and sat within two inches of him. The guide asked if he would like to feed him, as he was in a good mood. I'll let him finish the story.

"He was huge and I offered him three oranges and he gently brushed my skin, as he took them. He peeled them all and then ate one segment at a time. It was an amazing feeling just to be there."

Mike also had a lucky escape, after being taken ill in the jungle. He fell into a crocodile infested river. It was an horrendous trip to a hospital.

While in Indonesia, he even went back to school teaching for a short time. When he left, all the 400 pupils shook his hand. 'Mr Mike' had been the star attraction. It was Carisbrooke all over again.

Gary Rowett

I HAD A LOT OF TIME for football manager Jim Smith and I interviewed him a few times when he was the manager of Portsmouth. In January 1997, when he was managing Derby in the Premiership, I contacted him to see whether I could interview one of his players, on the eve of their game at Southampton. At that time, young Gary Rowett, once of Gurnard Youth, was the only Islander playing in the Premiership. Jim, as ever, was very helpful and I ended up in a Fareham hotel on a Friday night, interviewing Gary.

When I initially wrote this chapter, in January 2018, exactly 21 years on from interviewing Gary, he was the very successful manager of Derby County. Neither of us would have predicted that. Now that's all changed. He's moved to relegated Stoke City, where he hopes to achieve his dream of becoming a Premiership manager. Before I interviewed him in 1997, he'd played for Cambridge United and Everton, plus a loan spell at Blackpool. After over 100 appearances for Derby, he subsequently played for Birmingham, Leicester City and Charlton. His managerial career included Burton Albion and Birmingham City, before Derby. The Blues were crazy to get rid of him.

Gary could remember me writing about his father, Eric Rowett, who played professional football for Blackpool, in my *Sports Personality* column in the IW *Weekly Post*. Eric came here to work for the prison service and later moved to the mainland and eventually became a prison governor at Norwich.

When I was a pupil at Cowes Secondary, we had coaching visits from Pompey player Bill Thompson. In Gary's era, it was completely different.

"When I was at Cowes High, our football team had a great run in a national cup competition. Also in that team was Lee Bradbury (who is also featured in this book). Neither of us were the best players in that side. During the cup run, I was actually spotted by Cambridge United."

While at school, Gary had played for the junior sides of both Newport and Cowes. For a while he played in the same Newport FC senior team as his father who, locally, had played for Northwood and Cowes.

Gary was all set to go to Highbury College, Portsmouth, on a recreational management course, when he got the call up for an apprenticeship at Football League club Cambridge United. In the end, there was just once place available, with two Island youngsters vying for it. Gary was the lucky one.

His success at Cambridge, who'd moved him from a forward to a defender, meant the likes of Norwich and QPR were interested. When the Canaries manager, Mike Walker, moved to Everton, he signed Gary from Cambridge.

"It was a bit nerve wracking and I was a little overawed. I kept an open mind and was keen to learn. I'd played a lot of games at Cambridge and thought I should be playing in the Everton team. I was a little naive. I then played four games and felt I was a part of the first team squad.

"Then Mike Walker got the sack and Joe Royle came in. I was just another youngster surplus to requirements and was delighted when Derby came in for me."

He was suddenly playing against the likes of Alan Shearer, Eric Cantana and Ian Wright. He was thrilled to play at places like Highbury.

He'll never forget those years on the Island. "It's not until you leave that you realise just how great a place it is. I spent my school days and teenage years there and really enjoyed it."

CHAPTER 80

Michael Grade

IN 2012 MY PARTNER, Roberta Crismass, came up to London with me for a day out. I was due to go to the Wise Buddah Studios, in Great Titchfield Street, to interview Mike and the Mechanics. On our way down from the studio, I noticed a very smart looking guy in the reception area. Much to my surprise, they spoke to each other. It was, in fact, Lord Michael Grade. Roberta worked in Yarmouth Pharmacy and Michael was a regular visitor to the town and was about to buy a property there. He also often went into the shop.

I never miss an opportunity and she introduced me to Michael. Within a few weeks I was interviewing him in the Royal Solent Yacht Club, on the day he opened The Old Gaffers Festival.

The Grade family virtually ran British showbusiness for many years. The three brothers had arrived around 1910 as refugees from the Ukraine. Michael was the son of Leslie Grade and Lew and Bernard were his uncles.

Michael bided his time to join the most famous theatre agency in Britain. He began life as a trainee sports reporter on the *Daily Mirror*, thanks to a word from his father. When he went for his interview, for his £10 a week job, his father arranged for him to arrive in a chauffeured Bentley. Seven years later he joined the family business, when his father was seriously ill.

Eventually, Michael became a top agent, due to working with Billy Marsh. He went on the discover so many artists who become huge stars.

"I always remember when Larry Grayson's manager rang up and asked me to go and see his comedian, who just needed a break. I saw him in a drag club and loved his act and immediately booked him for a Palladium variety bill. This got him on to television and he never looked back."

Michael went to see the unknown Freddie Starr and the Midnighters in a club and saw his potential as a solo act. He gave him a Royal Variety spot – and he stole the show.

Others who owe such a lot to Michael Grade, include Peter Noone, Sasha Distel, Olivia Newton-John and Roger Whittaker.

Michael moved into television with great success and was responsible for the success of so many shows. He also shocked the light entertainment industry by prising Morecambe and Wise from ITV to the BBC. Another surprise was when he also took Bruce Forsyth to the BBC.

I loved his story about one of his all-time favourite comics, Ken Dodd. Michael had to provide a bill for a Royal Variety Show, for the Queen Mother. The Queen did not want her mother to be out too late. Having Doddy on the bill was somewhat risky. He had been warned – but the show over-ran by an hour.

"I met the Queen Mother at a private event a few weeks later and we sat down for a chat. I apologised for the show running late but she told me it didn't matter, as she loved Ken Dodd. She also told me she loved television shows like *Miss Marple*, *Dallas* and *Dynasty*."

Michael, officially known as Baron Grade of Yarmouth, who does some brilliant television documentaries on light entertainment, is such a legend in the world of showbusiness. I was chuffed to be able to tell him something he didn't actually know.

Many years earlier, his uncle, Bernard Delfont, provided live entertainment for two Island cinemas, the Medina, Newport, and Commodore, Ryde. Among the famous acts he brought were the bands of Billy Cotton, Harry Roy and Ted Heath and celebrated singer Richard Tauber.

CHAPTER 81

Steve and Helen Reading

DURING MY 17-YEAR SPELL as the organiser of the Isle of Wight Amateur Theatre Awards, which began thanks to Brian Dennis and Robin Freeman at the *County Press*, for an obvious reason, I tried not to show favours to any local amateur company. Hence, I never accepted invitations to after-show parties and other events. I had loved the job but it had become a one-man band, with no sponsor, and I was personally losing money. I decided to call it a day and create the time to write books. I missed it but one consolation was that I could then get closer to actors I'd admired, like Helen and Steve Reading, who have become friends.

I had great admiration for them when they formed their Red Tie Theatre Company. They gave young Islanders the chance to enhance their acting skills or, in some cases, actually just tempted them to give acting a try. Some of their productions were outstanding and I was often mesmerised by the performances of some of their young people. Before they began their own company, Helen had won many awards for her amazing acting skills, with the Apollo Players. Then Steve appeared more on stage and had his own much deserved success. On several occasions they acted against each other in plays and had more on stage rows and arguments than they ever did at home.

On one occasion, I went to see a Red Tie adult production, about a goat. It was a bold venture but did not appeal to me. I knew, after a few minutes, it could never win an award. When Bertie took out my interval bar of white chocolate, I told her I would eat it at home with a cup of coffee. She didn't like the play but was shocked I was going to leave. Actually, it was a relief for her.

I said we would creep out during the interval. No such luck. Helen was right outside for a quick fag break. She was not upset at all and just said: "Not your type of play then. We'll see you at the next one."

A year or two later, I was delighted to find out that both her and Steve had actually walked out of another amateur company's production. I felt a lot better.

When I'd finished hosting the final IW Amateur Theatre Awards night at Shanklin Theatre, I just wanted to walk away quietly, with no fuss. Mr Reading had other ideas. He suddenly appeared from the wings with a red book. It took me by surprise, as he and Helen had just received my final award for Services To The Island Amateur Stage. In past years, around the Island, I'd caught a few out with red book surprises and now the role was reversed.

I had tears in my eyes, as if I was watching *Call The Midwife*. Apparently, my family and friends were in on this. I stood there in shock and listened to my life story. I didn't know why the audience kept laughing, until someone shouted "it's behind you." It was a different kind of pantomime, as there were pictures of me throughout my life. In some, I even had hair.

After the evening, I realised just how gratifying it was to receive my own red book. Steve and Helen, who have both worked in the Island's educational system, had always appreciated just how much work went into watching over 50 shows a year. They all had to be analysed and the gala evening had to be meticulously planned and then hosted.

I still get regular invites to Red Tie productions and I always get that pre-show buzz of anticipation – and I've only walked out, just the once.

CHAPTER 82

Dick Taylor

I WAS LUCKY ENOUGH to have the local scoop that an original Rolling Stone had moved to the Island. He was not in their famous line-up that found world fame but Dick Taylor went back much further. He revealed the story of when they were schoolboys in Dartford, his mum used to supply Jaffa Cakes to Dick, his pal Mick Jagger and a few friends during their musical breaks. When Keith Richards joined them they became Little Boy Blue and the Blue Boys.

On July 12, 1962, the newly named Rolling Stones made their world debut at London's famous Marquee Club. That original line-up comprised of Dick, Mick Jagger, Keith Richards, Elmo Lewis, who later changed his name to Brian Jones, Ian Stewart and Mick Avory.

Dick reflected on those days: "We were just happy to be playing music and thought maybe we might do all right. Our R&B music was really suited to a minority audience. Trad jazz was the in-music of the time, after the early wave of rock 'n' roll."

They actually made a demo in those days and after 30 years it was discovered in a loft. Not Dick's, sadly. Christie's sold it for £50,000.

He was such a gifted artist and in late '62 Dick decided to leave the band to try and enrol at The Royal College Of Art.

"I've no real regrets and never really wanted to be a major pop star. I might have ended up like my good friend, Brian Jones, face down in a swimming pool.

"That hit me so hard. Also I always tell people I could have finished up being Bill Wyman. What a horrible fate!"

Eventually, Phil May tempted Dick into the music business to join the Pretty Things, where he played lead guitar instead of bass. They became famous – and not always for their music.

Dick suggested some of their antics were over-hyped, although they had their moments. Their publicity even suggested they made the Stones look like choirboys.

There was an incident in Wiltshire with a shot gun, produced by one of their over-protective roadies. They were also discussed by the New Zealand parliament and banned from the country.

Those of us lucky enough to see the amazing Ryde Commodore Sunday Concert in 1964, that, bizarrely, had Matt Monro on the same bill as the Pretty Things, will never forget the moment manager Reg Gammons pulled the curtain on the band. They played one song for over 11 minutes.

They survived and in recent years have appeared all over the world.

Young local musicians owe so much to Dick Taylor. He's lived on the Island for many years and has always been prepared to help budding musicians. He's always encouraged them to play music and has joined them on stage on many occasions. They look on him as a kind of godfather of rock. During the dizzy chart days of the Pretty Things he played in front of huge audiences. In more modern times he's been happy to turn up and play in local pubs like the Anchor, Cowes, and the Three Bishops in Brighstone, with aspiring young musicians.

"I love playing with local musicians. You can do what you want and not be expected to do a certain set. There is more room to experiment."

I once saw him augment a Rolling Stones tribute band in Ryde. He clearly loved it and so did the punters.

CHAPTER 83

Carol Laidler

IN MORE RECENT YEARS Carol Laidler has been synonymous with the success of the Island's First Act Theatre Company, who, in 2017, appeared in their 50th production. Carol and her team have been so productive in enhancing the lives of so many of our adults with learning difficulties. I've been so privileged to have seen virtually all of their shows and have witnessed the amazing progress made by so many of her clients. I've shed more than a few tears, as have many of their regular audiences.

Carol first came to the Island in the '70s, as a member of the Kay Jays dancing troupe, who were featured in three Sandown Pavilion summer shows, starring Bobby Dennis and Don Smoothey. They were brought to the Island by the late Don Moody, the much respected entertainment's manager for the theatres run by Sandown and Shanklin Council.

As a 13-year old, Carol went to the Arts Educational Stage School. Later, four girls from that school helped to form the Kay Jays. I'm sure Carol once told me she was known as Coral Penfold, due to a spelling mistake, when she appeared in a Norwich pantomime, with Ronnie Hilton. She kept the name for a while.

When we first met, Carol told me they had been lucky to be always in demand and had enjoyed three years of non-stop work. Their biggest thrill was to be the very first dance troupe to win TV's Opportunity Knocks. They also appeared in two all-winners shows. Other highlights included a residency at Bristol's Ashton Court Country Club.

While on the Island, Carol fell in love with a local rugby player, Alan Laidler, who once appeared in my *Weekly Post* Sports Personality column. They were married and settled in Sandown.

Just about ten years after she retired from being a professional dancer, Carol revealed to me that she had a real regret. "I wish I had danced for longer," she rued.

In 1984 she made a comeback to play Maggie in the Sandown Amateur Operatic Society's production of Brigadoon. She also became very involved with the Island's Keep Fit Association. I also saw her perform in some brilliant shows in Bembridge, for Good Intents.

Carol founded First Act in 1994 to aid students with learning difficulties. Initially, they just had 12 members. How times have changed. They now have groups that meet every Monday and Tuesday at Shanklin Theatre. They also have increased their shows to a two-night run, to enable all their members to take part.

My good friend Melvyn Hayes has become very involved with the group, as their patron. He's been so impressed with what he's seen and quietly told me that one member, in particular, was better than some professionals he'd seen. I would second that opinion.

In 2010 the future of her group was in real danger, due to a change of funding. Carol, their co-ordinator, and Vivienne Howell, as a director, formed First Act 2011, to save the day.

Their members are visually so excited when they are on stage and often don't tell their parents and friends what parts they are playing in their pantomimes and other varied productions.

"First Act 2011 is really a dream come true and I hope we can make it work," said Carol, in March 2011. They have certainly achieved their dream.

"There are no egos in our group. They are happy to be stars in one production and in the chorus for the next," enthused Carol. That is so noticeable in their amazing productions. I just congratulate every single person I have ever seen in First Act shows.

CHAPTER 84

Dave Kennett

WHEN I INTERVIEWED Yarmouth Lifeboat legend Dave Kennett for *The Beacon*, I had to spread it over two issues, to accommodate his eventful life both on and off the sea. Such a fascinating character, with a very soothing personality. I imagine when he was coxswain of the lifeboat it could be quite different, as he inspired his crew to daring rescues. As a tribute to him, as he's now retired, I'm going to recall some of them.

On the night of the 1987 hurricane they battled in force 14 winds. While most of us were hiding under the duvet, Dave and his men set sail to head to a call out, via the Needles. The 70 foot waves over the lighthouse meant they had to change plans and head the other way, for Bembridge. There, both lifeboats stood in readiness to help a ship three miles off St Catherine's and being blown towards the shore. Luckily, the tide changed and the ship's crew got her out of trouble.

On another occasion, two years later, again in hurricane conditions, Dave and his crew went to a rescue off Swanage Bay. It was a RoRo ship carrying Skoda cars and tractors that was in great danger.

"We were 18 hours on that job and when we took two chaps off, the wind had dropped to force 10. It was quite dangerous and the boat was at an angle and the others were rescued by helicopter, as she was about to roll over."

Dave was awarded a silver medal for a much publicised rescue, when they picked up five London policeman, at 3-30am, 14 miles south of the Needles. The huge waves filled the wheelhouse of the lifeboat.

In '83 the lifeboat was picked up like a cork, off Brook, and almost capsized in a force 11 – and she tipped 115 degrees.

Over the years Dave became quite a celebrity. In 1994 he was caught by Michael Aspel for a *This Is Your Life*. It was such an emotional evening and the five rescued London policemen all turned up. Six years later he went back to appear at *The Night Of A Thousand Lives*, to celebrate those given the famous red book. He also went to Buckingham Palace

to receive his MBE from Prince Charles. Another accolade came when he attended the 1976 Britain's Man Of The Year lunch. This was for his bravery.

True to form, behind every successful man is a very important lady. Dave has received such great support from Zoe, his lovely wife. She was always apprehensive when he rushed across the road on a stormy night to action a call out.

I had to go back in time, to catch him out. Fresh from his world trips with the merchant navy, Dave eventually bought a pleasure launch called Flamingo. This was the beginning of Kennett Marine Services. For some reason, Dave forgot to tell me about his initial voyage from Christchurch, where he'd picked up the boat, to Yarmouth. Rumours suggest he ran out of fuel and began to drift. You can guess what comes next. He had to call out the Yarmouth Lifeboat. I wonder what their coxswain, Harold Hayles, had to say about that?

I would have loved to have watched Dave drive a powerboat at 85mph through both gaps in the Needles. He has always loved a challenge.

Whenever I donate money to the RNLI, I always think of Dave and all our Island lifeboat crews, past and present. I must also mention the brave guys from Bembridge Lifeboat. Otherwise, I'll get banned from their posh headquarters.

CHAPTER 85

Roger Holmes

ROGER HOLMES can turn up at the most unexpected places and I'm no longer surprised when or where are paths cross. It's been at Fratton Park, where he introduced me to some of my schoolboy football heroes, like Ernie Butler and Len Phillips, playing the piano in Ventnor's posh Royal Hotel, conducting a local theatre orchestra and taking a funeral service at the Wootton Crematorium.

We might have never met, if he hadn't been rescued from a Godshill slurry pit, when he was just five years old. At Moor Farm, he was playing in the fields and got chased by a cow and suddenly he was up to his neck in a slimy mess and could so easily have slipped under. Luckily, the farmer's young daughter summoned help and he was saved. Apparently, he had to wear some of her clothes home. I promised him, on one occasion, I would not mention a particular garment. I won't break my word. Oh knickers! It doesn't matter now. I can assure you, he's only worn a pair just the once. Unless, he's got some with Portsmouth Football Club on the back!

Music has been such a great part of Roger's life - and it all began with piano lessons, when he was just six. It was much safer than a slurry pit! Later he took up the trumpet and played in local concert bands. He's also recorded his own solo albums of piano music, which even reached America. I will never forget the day I went to his Ventnor home to meet the legendary football star Derek Dougan, who was staying for a day or two. 'The Doog' was also a really good crooner. I was pre-recording a spot with him for my Sunday chat show. Would he sing to close the interview? Yes he would – and we didn't have far to go for a pianist. What a day that was – Derek Dougan and chocolate biscuits. Sadly, Derek died much too young.

Roger is so diverse in the many roles he performs. Whatever he does, it's always with a calm and easy manner. He doesn't relish the limelight and people respect him so much for this.

When Roger's parents had their 25th wedding anniversary party he was asked to say a few words but, at that time, he was not accustomed to making speeches and backed out. Ironically, the very next night his life changed for ever.

Roger told me: "I had to conduct my very first concert at the Bembridge Village Hall, in front of a full house. I also had to compere the show and could not get out of it. I was so surprised to find it quite easy and have never looked back since."

Then came another huge test. His friend, Jill Locke, asked if he could be the toastmaster at her son's wedding. It was a year away and so he reluctantly agreed to do it. Then, while playing piano at the Royal Hotel, Roger met a guy who was the secretary of the National Association of Toastmasters. He eased Roger's fears and even persuaded him to go on a five-day course. The wedding was a success and since then he's worked at Goodwood, Wentworth Golf Club and the Portsmouth Guildhall.

Roger Holmes is a very caring person. In 2017 I had to conduct a funeral service at Wootton Crematorium. When I got to the lectern, I spotted a good luck message from him. It was just what I needed.

CHAPTER 86

Eddie & Gloria Minghella

I ALWAYS THOUGHT Edward and Gloria Minghella were the perfect dream couple. They both had humble beginnings and certainly earned all the success that eventually came their way. Together, they built a world famous ice cream business, had five children, that any parents would be proud of, spent years working for the community, helped numerous local charities and, of course, were seen in Hollywood movies.

I interviewed them as a married couple and as individual local characters. I loved being in their company. Sadly, Gloria died in 2014 but I still enjoy my occasional visits to Eddie's home. Such a fascinating man to talk to – and his coffee is far superior to any made by those world famous names that have spread like a plague in recent years.

I still love the story of how they first met. In 1947 Eddie made his first-ever visit to the Island. At the time, he was working for an ice cream manufacturer in Portsmouth. In fact, he only came here because his boss asked him to visit. He had a son who was courting a girl from Glasgow, who now lived in Ryde. Her father had left them for another woman and her mother had moved to the town and opened a small business, called the Mayfayre, opposite Woolworths. The lady had three daughters and the youngest was 17 year old Gloria. Eddie's role was to help them get straight after their move.

"That trip cost me 2/7d (less than 15p today) and I was told to get out of the lounge on the paddle steamer, as I only had a second class ticket. I sat outside in the rain," said Eddie.

When he met Gloria, it was love at first sight. I don't think she quite felt the same way. She shook hands with the mainland visitor and thought no more of it. He came back on Christmas Eve and went to the Ryde Town Hall dance, with the rest of the family. Gloria stayed behind to look after the business, until a friend, John Valvona, arrived to take her to the dance and on to mass. There was a late night party back at the Mayfayre and at the end of it, Gloria and Eddie were left on their own.

"I was fascinated by this man who'd had such a deprived upbringing, with no real education. He could recite A *Tale Of Two Cities* and knew a lot about literature and I was keen to learn. When he found out John was not my boyfriend, he asked me out on a date. It was a New Year's Eve dance at the Commodore – and we are still together. We still have the same regard for each other. Nothing has changed, despite the ups and downs of life," reflected Gloria, back in 2012.

What a bargain for Eddie Minghella! A lifelong wife and partner for just a 15p ferry fare. It was worth getting wet for. Especially, as Gloria was once heard to mention that she could never marry an Italian. Incidentally, Eddie was actually born in Scotland, which might surprise a few people. He did spent some of his early years in Italy.

"Gloria and I were more than just man and wife. We shared everything together," said Eddie, one of the nicest men you could ever care to meet.

I once did a talk for one of Gloria's charities and they were both there. They had been such a comfort to me when my wife died. I had my new partner, Roberta, with me. They were delighted to meet her. I heard Gloria say to her: "You have a hard act to follow but you're doing well."

CHAPTER 87

Stuart Peters

STUART PETERS is one of those people you love to see walk into a room, whether it's at a rugby or croquet club, an Island country pub, or, in the old days, just to fit a new alarm system. Life has always been fun for Stu and his antics have created much hysteria. I'll mention a few in this chapter.

I once had Stu live on my radio show. What a combination that proved, with him and Stratford Johns, from TV's *The Bill* and *Barlow*.

When I last interviewed Stu I had quite a shock before I'd even got close to his Wootton home. I'd discovered he was actually winning local croquet tournaments. He'd already proved it was the perfect game for apprentice wrinklies. It also took a little less energy that playing over 500 local games of rugby. He finally retired from the Isle of Wight rugby team at the age of 48. He'd started playing the game for Ryde School and then the Saunders-Roe Apprentices. Years earlier, I'd seen his dad playing hockey for Saunders-Roe.

Stu, or Wally, as some call him, has a fund of great stories – some printable and some not. On a rugby club tour he was in the party who went to a London strip club, which was not a surprise. He obviously didn't take the advice that it's often dangerous to sit in the front row, particularly if you fall asleep. In his case, he was a bit bored, having seen it all before. One or two of the strippers were not too amused.

"One really took offence and came over to wake me up, but I can't tell you with what," teased Stu.

On another occasion they were playing rugby at New Milton and Stu was watching a ladies hockey match on an adjoining pitch, with his back to the rugby kick-off. When they sent a huge kick back to full back Peters, his eyes were still elsewhere. He heard his name being called out, turned around and caught the ball.

During another mainland visit he'd, unfortunately, had a row with his girlfriend, now his wife, and missed the Yarmouth ferry. He raced to Cowes, caught the Red Jet, changed into his gear in a toilet on the train to New Milton and just made the kick off.

The '70s were great days for the Isle of Wight Rugby Club and much of it was due to one man – and Stu was keen to thank him, publicly, in an article I was writing for *The Beacon*.

"Roy Jones was the real instigator. We won things like the Havant Sevens due to our superior fitness. He was such an inspiration to the players." Sadly, Roy died a couple of years after the article.

On the rugby field, Stu could virtually play anywhere. Either full back, scrum half or centre. Roy Jones advised him to settle as a scrum half. Stu later regretted he didn't act on his advice.

Malcolm Keith, one of his old rugby skippers, tempted him to try croquet at the Ryde Lawn Tennis and Croquet Club. He quickly picked up the game and was soon winning trophies. He has become particularly good at golf croquet and the club travel all over the south of England.

Many will remember Stu as the Island's Chubb alarm and security man. Once again, he proved such a popular character. He did a lot in shops and you could always hear his laugh, long before you saw him.

I'm told, he enjoys croquet better than strip clubs and has yet to fall asleep playing the game. If he did, a mallet would soon wake him up!

CHAPTER 88

Roy Pridmore

WHEN I WAS A SCHOOLBOY in East Cowes virtually all the Vics football team were my heroes. Roy Pridmore, a brilliant centre half, was among them. What an inspiration he was, particularly as he was also one of the finest batsmen on the Island.

His sporting life ended on November 17, 1958, on his 24th birthday. From that day onwards, he has never walked again. Since then, his inspiration has been of a different kind. He has just got on with his life from a wheelchair.

Before his tragic road accident, I had the thrill of playing cricket with him for J S Whites. Us youngsters idolised him and were so envious when he scored a century on three consecutive days. Island cricket history was made on 5, 6 and 7 August, 1957.

When I went to his home in 1999, to interview him for the *County Press*, I had quite a shock. Roy had turned his early boat building skills into making fantastic dolls houses.

Roy played football for Hampshire Youth and was the only player in their side that was not on the books of a professional club. They got to the final of the all-England competition. Locally, he also played for Sandown and Cowes. He also had cricket trials for Hampshire.

On that fateful November night, in 1958, Roy had played a Hampshire League match in Winchester and in the evening took his girlfriend, Shirley, who later became his wife, and two friends to the dance at the Winter Gardens. After dropping Shirley off in Ryde, he had that horrendous accident on the outskirts of the town.

"I've never been able to remember that accident and there were no witnesses," reflected Roy. For almost two weeks he was unconscious at Stoke Mandeville Hospital.

"When I finally came round I just laid there wondering how I was going to live. The first thing I heard was a cricket commentary from Australia."

Roy was bedridden for three months and was moved every three hours for comfort. He got to recognise Shirley's footsteps coming down the corridor. That was an unprescribed tonic and so were visits from mates and other family members. It was a tough internal personal fight for him. He became so low, being permanently paralysed from the waist down. When two of his hospital pals gave up their fights and committed suicide, he became even more distressed.

Back on the Island, our two fierce football rivals, Cowes and Newport, played a special match in aid of Roy. He was brought back to see the match and was so grateful to both clubs.

There were happier times ahead and Roy and Shirley got married in 1960. Then they had another two setbacks. Roy lost his job at J S Whites and Shirley lost the child she was expecting. Luckily, that Pridmore spirit saw them through. Friends rallied round and Roy was offered work at the IW Health Authority and stayed until he retired at the age of 58.

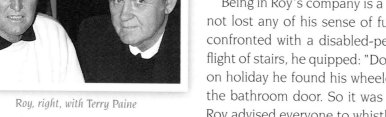

Roy, right, with Terry Paine

Being in Roy's company is a unique experience and he's not lost any of his sense of fun. On one occasion, when confronted with a disabled-persons loo, looking down a flight of stairs, he quipped: "Do I go from here?" Then while on holiday he found his wheelchair would not go through the bathroom door. So it was taken off for the week and Roy advised everyone to whistle, just in case.

I was embarrassed to find out he even decorated rooms from his wheelchair – and was far better at it than I was.

On one occasion, my good friend, footballer Terry Paine, was delighted to meet him.

CHAPTER 89

Kenneth Kendall

IN 1990, I WAS SO DELIGHTED when Kenneth Kendall moved to the Island. He was to many of us, a real newscaster – and not an autocue reader. He also would certainly not have earned such a ridiculous BBC salary as some of his less talented successors. There was no hint of an ego and, I know from our interviews, he frowned on some of his colleagues who became famous celebrities via light entertainment shows.

I have two special memories of Kenneth, who appeared live on my radio show soon after moving here. Following one live Sunday show, I had to rush to Newtown Church to undertake a reading at a special celebration service for the IW Hospital Radio, where I had started in 1974. I arrived about five minutes before I was due in the pulpit. As I was about to read from the Bible I noticed a famous face in the very front row, just inches away from me. No pressure then! It was Kenneth Kendall, who was a president of the local HBA organisation. In a strange way, I think he inspired me and I knew I couldn't make a mistake.

The other occasion was in September 2006, when he was so kind to me. Heather had tragically died and I needed to get back to work as quickly as possible after the funeral. It had also been a last wish from her that I kept up my interviewing.

Kenneth was an obvious choice, as he was such a great professional – and a friend. Thanks to him, I managed to get through it and I felt ready to meet Jim Davidson and Jane McDonald.

Kenneth actually came here to retire – or so he thought. He quickly opened a popular restaurant with his partner, Mark Fear, and then a world famous Cowes art gallery, where you could buy paintings from £150 to £50,000. These were from the gallery or via the internet. So sad to think that both are no longer with us.

I could listen to his BBC stories for hours. Some were very serious and others more light relief. His milestones included being on air when Russia launched the very first Sputnik. There were also tragedies he had to announce. The Staines air crash was such an emotional moment for him. It happened while he was reading the news.

"I also had some embarrassing moments. I think the worst was when one of my teeth actually fell out when I was reading the news. On another occasion, I could hear the phone ring but couldn't find it. It was in a drawer."

He did have a stalker. She never followed him but sent a fan letter every week for 25 years. The first one was a marriage proposal and he made the mistake of answering it, with a polite refusal. She asked him constantly for the next 25 years – and then gave up.

Treasure Hunt was a programme he enjoyed making. The public never realised he was often as much in the dark as the contestants. Many of us guys just envied him for working with Anneka Rice.

Kenneth's first-ever visit to the Island was in the early '60s, when he stayed at the famous Gloster Hotel in Cowes. He was a regular visitor and it was no surprise that he chose to retire here. Walking his dogs across the downs was always one of his great joys.

During his 22 years here Kenneth did so much for local charities.

CHAPTER 90

Josie Morey

WHEN I WAS A TEENAGER in East Cowes, one of the town's most feared young tough guys was Cyril Morey. He lived about four doors away from my grandmother and I always said hello when I walked past him. Occasionally, he managed to mumble a reply. I used to think no one will ever tame him. Then a miracle happened. He met Josie Woodhouse, a former Dr Barnado's baby of mixed race, who was living in Ryde with her local foster mother.

For both of them, it was the meeting of a lifetime. They have been happily married for over 50 years and simply are a dream couple. I first got to really know Josie when I interviewed her for my radio show. I went to their East Cowes home and quickly had one of the greatest surprises of my life. That very same Cyril Morey brought in the tray of coffee and cake, with a huge smile on his face. Who would have thought it?

Josie deserved such happiness, after the early race problems she was forced to endure. These even happened here on the Island.

In London, her birth mother had to leave Josie locked indoors while she went to work and her crying alerted neighbours. The local nursery schools had notices outside of their premises stating "no coloureds allowed." This led her to be moved to a Woodford children's home. I became quite emotional when she revealed stories of those days.

"I hated Saturdays when we were all lined up and people came to choose the children they were going to give a home to. Apparently, I was judged unplaceable and just saw so many of my friends being taken away.

"One day I saw this lady on a visit to the home and I did my little girlie routine in front of her. Two weeks later she came back and I tugged her sleeve and pleaded with her to take me. That lady was Ida Hill and she brought me to the Island. She was Miss Hill and they allowed her to foster me, as she was a Christian lady of good means."

It was a match made in heaven. Josie got to love her and Ida gave her a wonderful upbringing. She also had four doting aunts and later a very special school friend, called Sylvia.

Josie remembered that she had to go to a special meeting at County Hall, where they discussed whether she could even go to a local school. Thankfully, the decision went in her favour. That was not always to her advantage. A Sandown teacher took a dislike to Josie and, on one occasion, she was made to stand in the playground in the pouring rain, huddled against a wall. Luckily an observer spotted her plight and told her foster mother. Despite a meeting with the head, nothing was resolved.

By sheer chance, a Swanmore Middle teacher, she remembered as a Mr Card, heard of her plight and invited her to his school. On her first day there, her fellow pupils just wanted to touch her afro hair. Dr Barnardo's paid for them to move from Lake to Ryde.

When Josie met Cyril and they eventually became engaged, he had to go to London to be vetted by Dr Barnado's . He went back again when they wanted to get married.

Josie and Cyril have three children, Scott, Debbie and Julie, and eight grandchildren. They have enjoyed a life together that many have envied. What a thrill it was for her to become a very respected local magistrate and be invited to a Buckingham Palace Garden Party.

CHAPTER 91

Malcolm Smith

WHEN I FIRST MET the former king of Island roads, Malcolm Smith, I knew his voice more than his face, due to his regular appearances on Isle of Wight Radio. I eventually found his bungalow and there was not a pothole to be seen. I imagined it was one of the perks of an unenviable job. Everywhere he went, people wanted to talk about roads. It was not always friendly conversation, either. It even happened when he was eating out in a restaurants and pubs, with his lovely wife Alison.

I left the subject for some considerable time and knew he would be more happy talking about the Afton Pop Festival, Celine Dion, the IW Car Club, his rumoured Thomas The Tank Engine pyjamas and sports cars.

A career in chemistry was once considered as a possibility but he ended up at Ryde Borough Council, with a summer job, to see if he fancied civil engineering. That eventually led to a regular position, as a trainee engineer, with the IW River and Water Authority. In the summer of '70 Malcolm was sent to Afton Down. He was not lonely. There were half a million others and most of them needed water. En route, he even got special treatment. There was a one-way traffic system but when his van was spotted he got a fast police escort to the site.

"When Jimi Hendrix came on stage we were very close and actually stood on the side of the stage, holding on to the amplifiers.

"I did lose a colleague for a whole day and, apparently, there were problems with water leakage. Later, we found out the real reason. The ladies were washing naked under the taps."

Two years later Malcolm joined the IW Council, as a technician for highways. Later, for many years, he looked after road maintenance.

"I always had broad shoulders but always got the blame. If you were honest and smiled, they would listen to you."

Malcolm was often called out in the night for landslides, snow and floods. Sometimes it must have seemed he had a aura of doom around him, as he arrived at so many problem areas. These included the cliff fall behind the Shanklin Beach Hotel and the Undercliff Drive at Niton.

With regard to Niton he told me: "It started to move two days before and then later you could actually see the ground moving and hear the trees creaking as they moved towards the sea. One house had just been completely refurbished, including all new carpets. Eventually, it had to be demolished."

One snowy night at around 3-30am Malcolm and work colleagues were in County Hall sorting out major road problems. Suddenly, there was a knock on the front door and it was a party of young ladies who couldn't get back to the West Wight, after a disco night out. They let them sleep in the council chamber and finally got them home by a four-wheel drive vehicle.

Malcolm loved cars and when we last met he'd been the chairman of the IW Car Club for over 20 years. I know there was a sports car tucked away in his garage.

Between you and me, I discovered a couple of secrets. He was a closet Celine Dion fan and had been to Las Vegas to see her in concert. And, despite his famous Island accent, he was also part-Welsh.

Malcolm used to phone in to IW Radio's breakfast show, hosted by Andy Shier and Justine Field, from his bedroom. One day he locked himself in and had to get out of the window to get to work. Rumours suggested he was seen in his Thomas The Tank Engine pyjamas. I don't think he ever denied it!

CHAPTER 92

Eddie Walder

WHEN EDDIE WALDER was a governor at Camp Hill Prison, I managed to persuade him to bring one of his inmates, Jamie Lawrence, live into my Sunday lunchtime show. It all worked like a dream and Jamie sent a message to many of his fellow prisoners, who were all listening. It was not a clever way to grab extra listeners. It was a genuine attempt by Eddie and the Cowes football manager, Dale Young, to help Jamie go straight and become a professional footballer. He was released on Saturdays to play for Cowes. There was a happy ending and he ended up in the Premiership. Earlier this year they were reunited for Sky TV.

Eddie has always been that kind of caring person and has been an inspiration to many young Islanders. Not just in football, but also cricket and badminton. Many offenders who were in Camp Hill also owe a great debt to Eddie.

As a teenager, he went to Swindon Town, under their very shrewd manager Bert Head. Then he made a very brave decision and has never lived to regret it.

"I decided not to pursue my dream of a professional football career. I had a few self-doubts as to whether I was quite good enough. There were also a few other clubs interested but I returned to my job at Mew Langton's and then joined the prison service in 1976," said Eddie.

These days, non-league footballers show scant loyalty to their clubs. It's money at the end of the day. Thankfully, it was not always like that and Eddie was the perfect example. He played for Newport's first team as a 17 year old and didn't leave until he was into his 40s – and then it was to retire. He was once offered £10 a week to go and play for Salisbury, who were in a higher league. Ed turned it down and it's no surprise that he's still the club's leading goalscorer of all time.

At the old Church Litten ground he played in one of Newport's greatest forward lines of all time. It was Barry Dyer, Chris Cheverton, Barry Allen, Trevor Allen and Eddie. Four were Island boys, too.

Many still remember a Boxing Day match at Newport, when arch rivals Cowes were their opponents. There were a thousand or two inside the ground. Christmas derbies were always special and on that occasion Eddie and Cowes full back Dave Young left the game a bit earlier than the rest. Years later, when Dave came on my radio show, he was surprised when Eddie made an unexpected entry through the soundproof door. They'd been friends for years and there was never a return bout.

Whenever you meet Eddie, he's always such a pleasure to talk to and has a genial sense of humour.

For many years he played cricket for Newport, in a superb team. What a talented sportsman! At the age of 31, he started to play badminton for Whitecroft and won several Island Vets titles, in men's and mixed doubles, and was our county coach for over 20 years. While he was at Whitecroft they won the first division and Mallett Cup.

Ed was a one-club man in all his three major sports.

You never quite know where he'll pop up next. His son's father-in-law is fruit and veg king Derek Hunt and don't be surprised if you see Ed driving one of their vans.

I have kept in touch with Jamie Lawrence over the years and have been so proud of his achievements. Heather and I went to see him in London a few years ago and, thanks to Eddie and Dale, he'd fulfilled his dream.

CHAPTER 93

Chris Gardner

IN 1987 WHEN Chris Wilcox, the popular Sandown Pavilion stage manager, left the theatre, whoever took his place would have a hard act to follow. That man was Chris Gardner and he's proved the perfect choice. Popular with both artists and staff, he was there until they closed in 1998. What a sad day that was. Luckily, now he's at Shanklin Theatre, as technical manager.

Chris is a wonderful ideas man. In the early '90s he saw me struggling with one microphone, during my interviews he'd arranged at the theatre. Suddenly, he came up with a special Gardner one-off production of a double microphone stand. In other words, a mic at each end. It's still going strong and has been used in my interviews with Hollywood stars, world famous pop stars, a prime minister, royalty and many locals featured in this book.

Over the years Chris has revealed numerous fascinating theatre stories on my radio shows and given away a few secrets. Even a ghost story.

In 1991 Chris summoned me to Sandown Pavilion. Two of the summer show cast, John Martin and Marc Duane, had been terrified by a late night ghost.

Chris remembers it well. "I was locking up when I heard shouts from John and Marc and they were really scared. They'd just witnessed a screaming ghost walk through the gauze and the heavy safety curtain.

"A few years later, when I saw John Martin again, I asked him if it was just a publicity stunt. He said no. They'd really seen a ghost."

Apparently, two night watchman had rushed into the theatre with sticks, after hearing all the noise. I covered the story for both local and national newspapers and, late one night, even went there myself. Sadly, I never made one of Fay Baldwin's ghost story books.

When Chris first arrived at Sandown, he'd been the tour manager for Keith Harris and Orville. Ironically, the first show he did at the Pavilion was the Keith Harris Show. On that occasion, someone else was packing all the gear away and jumping into the van.

Chris had mixed memories of the 1989 Jimmy Tarbuck summer season, when the fire damaged the theatre and, within a couple of days, the whole production was moved to Shanklin Theatre.

Over the years he's worked with so many star names but an Islander, also featured in this book, has always been high on his list of favourites. Crisco never fails to make him laugh.

Chris has a fund of theatre knowledge, probably inherited from his parents, who always worked in theatres, including Sandown Pavilion. It's now a family double at Shanklin. His wife, Rebecca, is the stage manager. They see more of each other at work than they do at home. They are a perfect team.

When Chris first saw that Jethro and the Wurzels were coming to Sandown, he thought that Jethro was their new lead singer, as Adge Cutler had died a few years earlier. When they arrived, he admitted he'd never heard of Jethro. The Cornish comedian told him he'd been filling theatres for 17 years. Chris quickly found this out, as the big man returned so many times, in his own right, to fill the theatre. We both loved watching the grey haired old ladies arrive to see that lovely comedian from the Des O'Connor TV show. It wasn't quite like that – but they never had complaints.

Chris Gardner is another reason why Shanklin Theatre has been such a success. His experience and reputation, within the business, has proved so valuable.

CHAPTER 94

Billy Whittaker & Mimi Law

BILLY WHITTAKER and his wife Mimi Law were a popular comedy double act for over 20 years and favourites in numerous summer season shows all over Britain. They were also successful on the variety theatre circuits and in pantomimes. When Billy moved to Ryde, in the early '70s, to take over the role of Entertainments Officer for Medina Borough

Council, he had planned to give up the business. He quickly missed the live performing and went back to enjoy being one of the top pantomime dames. Stars like Norman Wisdom and Ken Dodd always wanted Billy in their Christmas shows.

They both had real showbiz backgrounds. Mimi and her impresario brother, Jerry Jerome, were Bisto Kids. Billy's father was one of Britain's top ventriloquists, who worked under the name of Coram.

I can remember going to the Kings, Southsea, in late 1975, to see Mimi in a pantomime that starred Hylda Baker. She went back a year or two later with Clodagh Rodgers.

When Sean and Caroline were growing up they looked on Billy and Mimi as extra grandparents and we went there for tea on numerous occasions. They loved it when Deryck Guyler and his wife Paddy came to stay.

When Billy was at Ryde Pavilion, quite often showbiz pals came over to see him and Mimi. On one occasion they rang my home to see if we could come down and meet Benny Hill. We were away on holiday at the time, which was a rarity in itself.

On the day Norman Wisdom appeared live on *John Hannam Meets*, I had to take him on to appear at a special function at the Frank James Hospital, in East Cowes. Then I had to take him to tea at Billy's Ryde home. That was a day to remember.

Bill was rated as one of Britain's top five dames. Once a young family member saw him on stage and was heard to say "that's Uncle Billy in a ladies skin."

He once told me the art of being a successful dame. " The most important thing is to play it as a man, children are very astute. You must not be seen as a drag act or female impersonator." How times have changed!

Billy and Mimi had a brilliant Cinderella sketch which they performed as if it was live on-air, at a radio station. It involved Mimi blacking out her teeth and causing complete mayhem.

When I had a television chat show on TV12, Mimi and I did a programme from Busy Bee in Ryde. It was a great success and she actually made up as the ageing Cinderella, in front of the viewers very eyes.

Billy was rather shrewd and I think he stopped an embarrassing moment for me, backstage at Ryde Pavilion. I was interviewing a rather passionate lady from their resident summer show, who I think, would have eaten me alive. She suggested we met in her dressing room, which was a little out of the way. Billy got wind of it and suggested we used an office at the top of the building, where other people were in view. Yes! I have often wondered what my fate might have been.

Many of us were so worried in 1985 when Billy was lucky to escape a serious M1 crash, involving 39 cars, in thick fog. He was en route to a pantomime season and had to be dragged from his burning car.

Sadly, both Billy and Mimi have taken their final curtain calls.

CHAPTER 95

Den Phillips

IN 1926 WHEN JOHN PHILLIPS moved to Compton Farm, from Barnsfield, near Yarmouth, the doctor gave him six weeks to live. It proved a hasty diagnosis and he went on to live another 30 years. It was just as well he did. Luckily, two years later his ninth child was born and many of us had the pleasure of knowing Den Phillips.

Life was not easy on their farm and in the summer they took visitors to make ends meet. Den and others lost their bedrooms for a few weeks and he was one of those billeted to the old caravan – after the chickens had been cleared out. Other than for those enforced seasonal breaks, he slept in the same bedroom for his complete life.

When Den, named after a Dennis lorry, left school he went to work for his father.

"Dad couldn't afford to pay us anything. He did let us shoot as many rabbits as we could and we kept the money as wages. That's why we didn't like anyone poaching. It was our wages they were stealing," said Den.

I loved his stories about poor old aunt Amy, who'd been jilted just before her wedding. Following this, she never left the farm for over 30 years. I'll recount Den's classic ghost story, in his very words.

"One night some visitors were convinced they'd seen a ghost. At midnight they spotted a lady with long hair carrying a gurt sack on her back, with a pig's head sticking out, and a huge carving knife in the other hand. They were quite scared.

"It was only Amy going out to feed her five dogs with a few animal heads we'd got from a Freshwater butcher. My mother didn't want them to know about Amy. So they went home thinking they'd seen a ghost."

Den rarely left the farm in his younger days – unless it was to get a haircut, three times a year, or go on rabbit safaris. He did break loose one night in 1956 and met a young lady called Jane Alder, at a young farmer's dance. Somehow, despite his lack of romantic skills, he asked her out. They found out they had nothing in common but got married the next year – and spent a lifetime together.

In the late summer of 1970, Compton Bay had a few more nudists than the one along the coast at Blackgang. Den and his cows loved every minute.

"I'll never forget the morning at the Afton Pop Festival when I had to queue to get down on Compton Beach. There were hundreds of naked women all over the place. There was no trouble and some sat down among my old cows, who seemed to enjoy it all."

Den's other great love was steam engines and his Easter Monday steam-ups drew hundreds of people. They flocked around him. On other Monday nights, Den often had a boys' night in, for a few mates. I have met some guys who went but they could certainly keep secrets.

He was such fun to be with but he had a wise old head. On one of the last occasions I met him he gave me a prediction. "In the future only the big farms will survive. It's so hard now for all the small men, with all this legislation." It is happening, just as he suggested.

CHAPTER 96

Ken West

JUST A DAY OR TWO after Ken West retired from 49 years on our Island railways, I invited him on to my radio show. He'd started as a cleaner in 1944 and ended up as a driver. You could instantly tell that he'd loved every minute. He couldn't get steam trains out of his blood and was going to help out at Havenstreet, where he would get the chance to drive some of his favourite old engines.

When Ken first joined, at Newport Station, everyone thought the steam trains would last for ever. Sadly, this was not the case. I can still vividly remember going on every train route on the Island. We would cross the floating ferry from East Cowes to Cowes, in the days when it was never off service, to catch the train at Mill Hill Station. From there you could get to Newport, Freshwater, Ventnor West, Sandown, Shanklin, Ryde, St Helens and Bembridge. Luckily, my father took home movies of some of our train adventures.

Ken was full of wonderful stories. How they served the quickest bacon and eggs on the Island – from the end of their coal shovel. There was a rumour they'd once cooked a pig. He didn't deny it.

I was lucky to be in the company of our Blue Riband train driver – and there was not an ocean liner in sight. Ken's voyage was from Ventnor Town to Ryde St Johns. He created a record of just under 12 minutes, with his light engine and two mail vans, returning to depot.

"Sometimes we had late night races. I drove from Ventnor to Ryde St Johns and my mate had the last train from Cowes to Ryde. Whoever was last home, bought the drinks in the pub."

Ken drove the last ever train out of Cowes Station, now the Marks & Spencer food store. It had six coaches and was filled to capacity.

"I felt very nostalgic about that final run, as I drove W24 *Calbourne* back to Ryde. A lot of men lost their jobs at that time and steam was being phased out."

On one trip to Newport, Ken had to stop the train because there was a cow on the line between Horringford and Merstone.

"I got down and chased this cow with a small wire brush. I don't know what I expected to do with that. I followed the cow for nearly half a mile and then when it got to the grass verge at Redway Bank, it turned and chased me," said Ken.

Ken also revealed the story of the tunnel between Wroxall and Ventnor. With local mist around and smoke from the last train still in the tunnel, you could sometimes get lost and not know when you were out. He had his own method.

"I counted 26 joints in (clickety, click and all that) and then if you looked at the dome of the engine you could briefly see daylight. That was the vent on to the downs above. Then, if you counted 36 more joints you knew you were out of the tunnel. That was very important, as there was a signal box just outside."

Ken could remember a Ryde to Ventnor run, when he had six coaches and up to 700 passengers on board. No time for eggs and bacon then. There was a steep climb up Apse Bank towards Wroxall, which tested the tiny engines. Making sure they had enough coal and water was a major factor.

In the cold winter of 1947 when the heavy snow arrived our trains were the only form of transport that was running. That was before Dr Beeching came along to end it all.

CHAPTER 97

Oscar Stretch & Nobby Nash

OSCAR AND NOBBY are well suited to share this chapter. On a Saturday night in 1990 they revealed a secret that has now become a kind of local folklore. When everybody's Island soccer hero, Roy Shiner, sadly died in 1988, Oscar and Nobby were asked to be pallbearers. They were the shortest and were advised to go at the front.

Oscar revealed the story: "I didn't own a suit and Nobby heard about this and kindly offered to loan me one. I went to his house and he had a wardrobe full of them. With him being rounder than me, it didn't fit that well. I just wore a belt and hoped for the best. As we walked into the church the trousers started to fall down and so I had to put one hand on them and the other on the coffin." Roy, who had a great sense of humour, would have loved that story.

Back in 1990, two years after the funeral, Nobby pleaded on-air for the return of his suit. It has still not been returned. What did Nobby think about that? I did take a recent picture of both of them wearing the famous suit, 30 years after Oscar borrowed it. That's the closest Nobby will ever get to it.

"I've seen that suit so many times. We've been to funerals of old football mates and various functions and he's always got it on. He thinks it looks better on him than it did on me," said Nobby.

In the '60s and '70s they were two of the most notorious players in Island League football. There was certainly no love lost when they played against each other. Like true Islanders, they were mates off the pitch.

Nobby has negotiated a few interviews for me. Being such a generous man, he even drove me to the homes of Mick Channon and Bob Champion. He loved being the chauffeur. When he was the delivery boy for his wife's florist business, sometimes, he took longer than it did to grow the flowers. He could talk for hours – and don't we know it.

In more recent years, Oscar became known for his amazing Christmas lights. He won awards for them and his garden blooms. Over the years he's raised £38,000 for local charities. Only health problems put out his Christmas lights.

My favourite 'Stretchy' story is when he saw the local paper headlines "Stretch Grabs A Brace." He told me: "I couldn't understand it. I've never worn anything on my teeth!"

On one occasion when Nobby was playing for Cowes against Alton Town, he didn't have a quiet Friday night. He got in at 3am, following a stag night, went to the wedding at lunchtime and played football in the afternoon. Apparently, it was one of his best games and he scored their only goal. Other than a couple of years at Cowes, Nobby played for Seaview. For several years, there was no Island League side to touch them.

Oscar Stretch

Nobby Nash

CHAPTER 98

Maurice Leppard

WHEN YOUNG WROXALL LAD Maurice Leppard attended Ventnor Secondary Modern he was the only boy in the commercial class. If he was teased by his local mates, he certainly had the last word – a few million times. Those shorthand and typing lessons led him to a career as one of the Island's top news journalists. In fact, he was a real hero to a young schoolboy like myself.

At the age of 16, he went straight from school to become a junior reporter at the *County Press*. The vacancy only occurred as his predecessor went off to do national service. He could type and do shorthand but had never answered a phone in his life. He blushed every time he nervously took a call.

When he joined, the front page was purely adverts, scandal stories were not deemed right for readers, by-lines were undiscovered and a political bias was not too hard to fathom.

He once told me: "As an office junior I was often sent to the undertakers to find out who had died. Then I had to interview the relatives and sometimes they invited me to see the body in the front room."

If Maurice was sent to Whippingham, to cover East Cowes Vics football matches, he had to borrow the secretary's bike to cycle to the nearest phone box and pray it was empty. Reporters earned a little pin money by phoning half-time reports to the two mainland sports papers, who had Saturday night editions sent to the Island. Sometimes when he'd got back to the match he'd missed a couple of goals.

When Maurice was called up for national service he was replaced by Roy Blackman, who went on to make Fleet Street.

Maurice came back to the CP and wrote a very popular cricket column, under the guise of 'Stumper.' We all knew who it was – and he was the wicketkeeper for Shanklin CC. In his very early days he was on huge money – about £1-75 a week. Some of that quickly went on a Jolliffe's pie. There were perks – like free tickets for Newport's three cinemas.

He left for a while to become a sports reporter for the *Surrey and Hants News* but, eventually, headed back to the Island and rejoined the CP.

Then in a bold move he decided to join the Newport office of the *Southern Daily Echo*, a Southampton-based newspaper selling 100,000 copies a day. No social media in those days. Some of us now realise just how lucky we were. When they closed their Island office, 25 years later, Maurice was their chief reporter.

They were golden times and the local *Echo* boys were also stringers for the national papers. There were huge national stories like the Parkhurst Prison riots, redundancy problems at Saunders-Roe, the *Pacific Glory* and *Tarpenbek* shipping tragedies and the legendary pop festivals.

"I was the fall guy for the 1970 festival. Fiery Creations gave me the scoop it was to be Alum Bay and the rest of the local media followed me with the news. This was just the cover story while they negotiated for Afton Down."

Maurice was also the very first Island-based radio news reporter. He voiced his daily *Radio Victory* reports as Bill Roberts. He was almost rumbled on one occasion.

When the Echo closed their Island office he went back to the CP. He spent six months compiling *Black On White*, the book on the story of our local newspaper.

After he retired, he became a constant letter writer to the CP. One of his comments about Charlotte Hofton made many people smile – but maybe not Charlotte.

Maurice was almost too nice to be a hard news reporter. He was such a gentleman and a role model for many others.

CHAPTER 99

Alan Johnson

WHENEVER I WENT to see a production by the Newchurch Drama Group, the first thing I did was to look at the programme to see if Alan Johnson was in it. When he was performing, you knew anything might happen. Like the night they trusted him with the interval raffle – and it was the funniest moment in the show.

Alan, who became a butcher by trade, was perfect for the job. He was never lost for words and helped brighten up everyone's day. For a redundant toolmaker, he finally made a success of his new career, after an initial problem when he got his red meats muddled. At Shanklin's Regent Street Butchers he was sent to the fridge to get some beef to put through the mincer, with the instructions it was long, red and round. Eagle-eyed Alan saw it straight away and within minutes it was in the window at £2 for a lb. Later the boss asked him where the fillet steak had gone. "What's it like?" said our trainee butcher. He was told it was long, red and round and sold at £10 a lb. That became a bargain day for shoppers.

Early in life, Alan had dreamed of RADA and perhaps a career in the theatre. He'd been successful in school productions. It was not possible. A few years later, he was actually on stage, at Shanklin Theatre.

"I loved it but it was hard work. I did *The Boyfriend* from the first week in July until mid September, six nights a week. I had my own shop by then and started work at 7am and worked until 5pm. Then I nipped home for tea and went straight to the theatre for the evening show."

After Alan closed his Shanklin shop, he was looking for a new challenge and became a volunteer courier driver for Island Volunteers. This proved a great motivation and the young people he drove enjoyed his endless fun and banter.

Eventually, he took a summer job with Safeway, Lake, which became Morrisons. It was for four months and he stayed for around 20 years, until he retired.

When the store was searching for an idiot, in the best sense, they looked no further than Alan. Who else would dress up as Pavarotti and go around the shop singing "just one sliced loaf."

Alan told me this story. "I was asked to go to the manager's office to let him see me, as he liked a laugh and wouldn't mind. I burst into his office and said 'I hear you're looking for a tenor.' Unfortunately, there was a rather serious meeting going on, so I decided this Pavorotti had to make a quick exit."

Customers also loved his Elvis impression but wondered where the sideburns were. They'd been glued on and fallen off.

I love the story of Alan's blind date at Yaverland car park. For Heather, the mystery lady, it was her third try. She'd run away from two others in Ryde. This time he ran off, which worried Heather, but he'd only gone to get the 12 red roses from his car. He, obviously, liked the look of her.

Heather took up the story, in case Alan was embarrassed.

"We walked up towards Culver Haven and halfway up he was taken short and had to pop behind a hedge. He was gone for ages and I thought he'd had second thoughts and cleared off. When he eventually came out, he said he was sorry but the flies had gone on his trousers," said Mrs Johnson. Yes, there was a happy ending.

I must tell you this. One night he was taking his finale bow in boxer shorts at Shanklin Theatre – and all was not safely tucked in. The play was called *No Sex Please, We're British*!

CHAPTER 100

David Griffiths & Danny Briggs

I'VE ALWAYS BEEN a great follower of Hampshire Cricket Club and was thrilled during my days on the *Weekly Post* to interview the last ever Island-born cricketer to play county cricket. Ryde's Bill Scott played for Hampshire in 1927. I never expected to interview two more in the following years but along came David Griffiths and Danny Briggs. Sadly, in the end, I don't think Hampshire were quite fair to either of them.

When I first met David, in 2005, he was not a pretty sight. He'd just returned from playing for the England under-19s on an Indian tour. The heat and food had taken its toll and he was thin, very pale and looked quite weak.

Cricket was a family tradition. His father, Adrian, played for Wales, his grandfather, Ron, starred for Shanklin CC and others in the cricketing dynasty included David Porter, Roley and Mark Ringer, Trevor Mew and his uncle Jonathan.

David told me during a later interview: "I used to go and watch Hampshire play and dreamed of playing in their team. I'm now lucky enough to actually play with some of those players."

I jumped for joy when he took 6 for 85 against Nottinghamshire at Trent Bridge – and he had several catches dropped. He was also in the Hampshire team that won the Clydesdale Bank 40 Final at Lords. The match changed when he got rid of England's Ian Bell. Griff could bowl around 90 miles an hour. In total, he took around 150 wickets for Hampshire in first class cricket. Sadly, injuries hampered his career and he moved to Kent CC before retiring from county cricket.

David Griffiths   *Danny Briggs*

On a memorable day at Chelmsford, against Essex, all the wickets Hampshire took in the day were by Islanders. Danny Briggs was also in that team.

Danny was such an icon for young local cricketers. He played for Ventnor CC, before joining Hampshire, and he went on to become the first Islander ever to play first class cricket for England. He also became the first young spinner, since Kent's Derek Underwood, to take 100 wickets in first class cricket. He once took 5 for 19 against Durham. He was outstanding in Twenty20 cricket and had such a knack of removing star names. In 2010 he helped Hampshire win the Friends Provident t20 Final. In the semi-final against Essex he was the man of the match. Briggsy also took 6 for 45 for the England Lions against the Windward Islands.

Many eyebrows were raised when Hampshire let him move to deadly rivals Sussex. For them, he has played more county cricket and also achieved his maiden century in the first class game.

The first time I interviewed Danny, when he made a guest appearance at Ventnor Cricket Club, they had a wiring problem with their electric plugs and the recording was not up to broadcast standards. To be on the safe side, he came into our radio studio the next day and all was well. A real confident guest.

I must say these two young men have been such a credit to the Island and our cricket fraternity. They are both so level headed and it's been such a personal thrill to follow their progress. We can be so proud of their achievements.

When I interviewed local cricketer Tony Millward, in 1986, he rued the fact there were no local youngsters coming through and how we particularly needed young bowlers. He was spot on. Thankfully, things eventually got so much better, as David and Danny have proved.

CHAPTER 101

Wally Malston

LONG BEFORE I MET WALLY MALSTON I'd heard local stories about a former Cowes dental technician who'd become a famous scriptwriter. He'd written gang shows for the local scout troop and entertained school pals for years. Wally had also appeared at holiday camps as a stand-up comedian.

Heather knew Wally from her early days in Cowes. I think one of her first boyfriends was one of his mates. One day we were shopping in Newport and she spotted Wally. By this time he'd moved to the mainland, become a professional and was writing for top comedy stars like Ted Rogers, Bob Monkhouse and Jimmy Tarbuck. He was a fast walker and we couldn't catch up with him. I was writing for the IW *Weekly Post* and was determined to hunt him down. Thanks to Island country singer Brian Munro, I was able to do just that. Wally's mother was still living in Cowes.

Wally came to our home for the evening and it proved a night to remember. He was such an inventive writer but known as a wee bit eccentric, which endeared him to us even more. He'd borrowed a car and it was not starting too well. Instead of leaving it on the road, which had a slight incline, he came down my drive and left it hard up against a fence. Later, we managed to get him away, eventually.

Wally revealed the story of how he decided to write to Bob Monkhouse, who, at that time, was compering *Sunday Night At The London Palladium*. Bob liked his one-liners and started to use a few.

"I kept sending jokes to Bob and he paid me £5 for every one he used. On Sunday nights I used to sit in front of the television and count up my fivers," said Wally.

Over the years Wally had great success and was involved in so many hit television shows with Ted Rogers, Bruce Forsyth and Jimmy Tarbuck. He even wrote material for top American stars, including Bing Crosby. His name was seen on the end credits of shows like *3-2-1*, *Play Your Cards Right*, *The Generation Game*, *Winner Takes All* and *Sunday Night At The London Palladium*.

When Heather and I celebrated our 25th wedding anniversary, Wally invited us to stay at his home in Fleet. He took us out for a meal on the Saturday night and the following day we were his guests at *Sunday Night At The London Palladium*. We sat in on the rehearsals, had tea with the company, met our old friend, Jimmy Tarbuck, and some of the show's stars, including Sinitta and Marti Caine. We saw the live show.

We loved being with Wally and were so shocked when he died in 1998. Sadly, we were with him in the Farnham Hospice the day before he died.

A week or two later we were at his funeral service at the Aldershot Crematorium. There were many stars there and Bruce Forsyth gave a fantastic eulogy. It was more like a stand-up comedy routine, all about Wally.

There was an exciting end to a very emotional day – and Wally would have been so thrilled. He'd been trying to get me an interview with Brucie for some time but we had never got together, as he was always so busy. Ted Rogers, a good friend, introduced me to Bruce and we instantly decided to do an interview and dedicate it to Wally. Bruce gave me his home phone number and told me to ring him in a few weeks, after he'd got back from the West Indies. True to his word, we got together. I went to his home, on the edge of Wentworth Golf Course. "Wally was more than my scriptwriter. We were great friends and he was such a sweet man," said Bruce.

What a great loss to showbiz when Sir Bruce died in 2017.

CHAPTER 102

Neil Shutler

OVER THE YEARS, whenever I've seen Neil Shutler, I've always thought of children, doughnuts, spin bowling and Al Jolson. Neil and his wife Dorothy produced ten children, on one memorable day he made 3000 doughnuts in his Nodehill bakery, over the years he took hundreds of wickets for Newport Cricket Club and he's always been the Island's greatest fan of the legendary American entertainer. I've never mentioned stocks and shares – but he has.

In 1946, when Neil, better known as Shutty, came out of the navy, he used the £2000 left him by his late grandmother to purchase the Newport bakery business of E. J. Caddy. Shutler's became one of the town's most famous businesses. It was a real gamble, with 15 other bakers in the town. Prior to the war, Neil had worked for Howard Harvey, in his high street bakery.

Neil's family business, eventually taken over by his son, Paul, certainly not a Jolson fan, was sold after over 50 years in Nodehill. Neil's first week's takings were just £37. He was a quick learner and realised he could take £200 on a Sunday, with not many other shops open.

Shutty has always had a fund of stories, some have been repeatable and others not. He's always been at his best when surrounded by some of his pals from Newport Cricket Club. He was a kind of mentor for many of the younger players. I'm sure he's led a few astray.

The girls from the school next door were the victims of a few of Neil's tricks. He used to place doughnuts in the playground, on pieces of string. When someone attempted to pick it up, he pulled it away. That prank would certainly not get by today's health and safety brigade.

Neil came on to my radio show and also appeared on my TV12 chat show. As the end credits started to roll, he was seen getting up to walk away. As he was still wired up, it would have been chaos. We should have put him on a doughnut string!

The story of how Neil met Dorothy is real Mills and Boon material.

He'd met Dorothy on a blind date (no dating websites in those days), arranged by a nursing friend of hers at Whitecroft Hospital. She'd described him as " a nice young man."

Neil told me the story. "I hid in a Newport shop doorway to see what I was getting. Suddenly, I saw this lovely redhead and I couldn't get across the road quick enough. Within a few minutes we were inside the Grand Cinema."

While walking home from Whitecroft, following that first date, he looked up at the moonlit sky and said to himself, "I'm going to marry that girl."

I once asked Dorothy about that particular night. "I thought he was a bit forward," was her reply. No surprise there, then.

I was thrilled to be invited to their Diamond Wedding – and they still looked a couple made for each other. Did she have any regrets? I was frightened to ask her.

Neil lived for his cricket. On match days he would start very early in the morning, have a few hours off for the match, and then go back to work. Once, during an evening time limit game, the equivalent of today's Twenty20, he suddenly remembered he'd left nine trays of meringues on the low oven. It was too late to worry and he used them as sugar for the next day's buns.

I began this chapter when Neil was 99 and have finished it when he reached 100. Loved the party – but there was not a doughnut in sight!

CHAPTER 103

Philip Norman

MANY SUCCESSFUL ISLAND JOURNALISTS have learnt their skills at the *County Press* and then moved on to mainland publications. One of our most successful, Philip Norman, was turned down by our popular local paper because they had no vacancies. He left Ryde quicker than expected and ended up writing features for *The Times*, *Sunday Times* and *Daily Mail*. He's also written books on Elton John, Buddy Holly, the Rolling Stones, John Lennon and Paul McCartney. His interviews have included Elizabeth Taylor, Richard Burton, Colonel Gaddafi, James Brown and Rod Stewart.

Quite an impressive track record for a journalist who readily admits to have suffered a miserable childhood growing up on the Island. Thousands have shared Philip's vivid disappointments via his best selling books *Skater's Waltz* and *Babycham Nights*.

I have met him on many occasions and also enjoyed his hospitality at his Hampstead home. He also arranged an interview for me with one of my great rock 'n' roll idols, Neil Sedaka. Philip wrote the book for a brilliant stage musical called *Laughter In The Rain*, which featured Neil's songs and his incredible story.

Back to Philip and his early Island days. "For me, it really was a time of severe misery and frustration, with not much happiness but a lot of humour."

He'd actually come to Ryde when his father, Clive, took over the Ryde Pier Pavilion, often known as The Seagull.

"I was ashamed to live in a derelict old pub in Castle Street, with my grandmother. She was a wicked old witch but very charming and like the head of a mafia family. In that house there was no hot water or proper toilet facilities, the walls were covered with mould and the sweet store was full of rats.

"My father was so unsuccessful and lived at the end of the pier with his girlfriend. This was supposed to be a secret but everybody knew."

Philip did enjoy life at Ryde School. His close pals there included Roger Peck and Mike Spooner. Local musician, Brian Sharpe, was also an important early influence. Later he wrote a brilliant television play called *Words Of Love*, which was based around that era and the birth of rock 'n' roll. It was inspired by Buddy Holly.

"On one occasion, I was embarrassed to find I was the only person in the school photograph without a blazer badge. Skipping some school uniform requirements allowed my father, who was a virtual alcoholic, to have more money for drink."

I can listen to his stories for hours. From that desperate life in Ryde, that could have so easily destroyed him, he later found himself on the set of *Where Eagles Dare*, talking to Richard Burton and Elizabeth Taylor. His other milestones include joining the Everly Brothers and Rod Stewart on their tours, spending 14 hours in the company of Yoko Ono and having the Beach Boys sing *Barbara Ann*, just for him.

Some people thought he was anti Paul McCartney and he now admits not being fair to him in his book called *Shout*, which was on the Beatles.

"When I did a book on John Lennon I got a message to Paul to tell him about it and said that he would probably not talk to me because of the back story of the two of us. I also told him I was not anti him.

"I actually got a phone call and the voice just said 'it's Paul here.' I wish I'd said Paul who? In fact, he agreed to answer my questions by email. Later on I asked him if I could do a companion book on him and got his approval."

How different might Philip's life have been if there had been a job at the *County Press*?

CHAPTER 104

Bernie Cullen

FOR MANY YEARS Newport's Bernie Cullen was seldom out of the public eye. He was the front man of famous Island band The Five Alive, the goalkeeper for Newport in the Hampshire League and was known to frequent a few local hostelries. His story included Princess Anne, Maigret, Martin Chivers, Manchester City and, much to my embarrassment, Dame Edna Everage. The last time I interviewed him, it was in his man cave bar, called Sinatra's.

Bernie would have thought I needed more than one page for his life story – and he would probably have been right. Mind you, I do have the censors to think about!

He originally sang with the Medina City Jazz Band, before moving on to The Five Alive. They had a large local following and took up a five year residency at the famous La Babalu Club. They were also spotted at a yacht club dance in Cowes. Bernie related this story the first time we ever met.

"We were invited to play at a posh ball at Burnham Beeches. I used to drop my trousers to reveal my red and white striped boxer shorts. I did just that and was then told Princess Anne was in the audience. I was given a Royal pardon and then I asked her if her old man was coming to Cowes Week."

On another occasion they were introduced to actor Rupert Davies, famous as TV's *Maigret*. They were also invited to make a demo record in London. The boys were not too impressed and, on the way home, threw most of them into the Solent. I did embarrass him one day by playing a copy that had survived.

They made a late '80s comeback, which, I admit, was on my suggestion. It proved successful and they supported the likes of the Tremeloes, Searchers, Brian Poole and the Fortunes. They then retired and later made one final comeback.

At one gig, I was called on stage to meet a famous Australian superstar. On came Dame Edna Everage, who had an uncanny resemblance to Bernie Cullen.

Bernie, who played for Hampshire Boys, with Martin Chivers, was a gifted goalkeeper and, this may not surprise you, was very flashy. On one very special occasion - he just couldn't stay on his feet. Luckily, it was after Newport had won a cup final at Fratton Park. Rumours suggest committee man Ollie Hamilton saw him home, opened the door, pushed him in and ran as fast as he could. I also always tried not to mention Manchester City – his favourite team. Oddly, he never said much about the other team in the city.

Bernie, who at one time was almost unbeatable at shove halfpenny, also raised so much money for local charities. Many of us admired him for the enthusiasm that had gone with it. Over the years, this very likeable guy, took stick from his mates but he certainly got his own back.

I must say that when he made live appearances on my radio chat show, I did sometimes wonder if it was a good idea. Especially, if he'd had a little refreshment en-route. In the end, I pre-recorded his conversations, just in case.

Seriously, I was eternally grateful to Bern. In 1990 he was the first-ever guest on *John Hannam Meets*. I'd been told on the Thursday that I had a live chat show on the Saturday night. Who could I get at short notice? Bernie came up trumps.

He was such a popular guy, as hundreds proved when they attended his funeral service in January 2018. They filled St Thomas' Church in Newport. So many of us miss him.

CHAPTER 105

Pam Bateman

AS SOON AS I SAW Pam Bateman on Cilla Black's *Surprise Surprise* I just had to interview her. Her appearance was so inspirational, as she'd been blind for quite a few years. Her personality was also just perfect for a chat show. A year or two later, after we had become good friends, Pam had a Cilla-type surprise for me. On the fifth anniversary of IW Radio, she decided to ask a presenter to fly in a plane with her. I opened the letter live on air and had no option but to agree to do it, despite being twice as old as any other presenter. Thankfully, she explained there would be an experienced pilot also in the cockpit. It was an Easter Saturday I will never forget.

Our flight from Sandown Airport was due for 11am. Just 30 minutes earlier, she'd been given a few brief instructions by the pilot. I didn't like flying and had remained on the ground for a few years, due to problems with Meniere's Disease, which causes inner ear problems. I didn't want to disappoint Pam, so I filled my mouth with boiled sweets and hoped for the best. Once I realised the real pilot was going to take off, I did feel a little more relaxed. I also had my portable recorder on board, so that my listeners could capture the atmosphere of the occasion.

We were up for around 30 minutes and there were some stunning views of the Island. I did close my eyes when I was told Pam was going to take the controls and we did sway around a bit – but all was well and she even helped to land the plane.

I had so much admiration for Pam. Her previous escapades, all for charity, included a parachute jump, a scuba dive at the West Wight Swimming Pool, a catamaran trip around the Island and driving a car at 75mph around Bembridge Airport. On Cilla's show she went down the bobsleigh run at San Moritz and millions shared her screams of delight as she clearly enjoyed every minute.

I know she did find the parachute jump, her first charity event, rather daunting.

"When I jumped out of the plane I felt really frightened. I was falling at 200 mph and could not see the ground or the parachute open. It was really scary but I would do it again because I know what to expect."

Personally, over the years, I have found many disabled people who were just a pleasure to be with. They have been so inspirational, with a real zest for life.

Pam gave me her thoughts: "I suppose everyone has down days, even young and fit people. I don't think disabled people need to say that they are. They just need to show their abilities. This is what I'm all about. I've now got more freedom since I got Patsy my guide dog and I can lead a more normal life."

For a while Pam lived in a unit behind Polars and when I popped in for a cup of tea, she always insisted on making it for me, as I was her guest.

I used to love seeing her in the street. I never told her who I was. I just kissed her gently on the back of her neck. She never failed to reply "that's you John Hannam." It wasn't sexual harassment – because I know she liked it!

I feel rather privileged to have known Pam Bateman – a real one off.

CHAPTER 106

Phil Mew

IN CRICKET TEAM DRESSING ROOMS there are always those who want to sit quietly in the corner, some want to entertain with a few stories and, occasionally, some want to talk about the match. There is always one hunky guy who wants to walk around with next to nothing on – until his pals tell him to cover up. The actual words are best left to the imagination. In Phil Mew's case – he ended up with Cilla Black on B*lind Date*.

Phil, such a successful pub owner in more recent years, particularly at the Fighting Cocks, Arreton, was a popular member of our Godshill team, who were lucky enough to win the Island Village League. He had no fear and with so many more mature guys in the team, was the butt of more than a few jokes. He had the last laugh when he came in and told us he had passed an audition for an 1987 appearance on B*lind Date*. Actually, he was a perfect choice. I never asked his mother and father, staunch Methodists, what they thought!

I think we were all delighted but, of course, didn't tell him so. We were disappointed when he was turned down, after proving a great television guest. How could a lady turn down Phil Mew? In fact, his segment was actually shown in T*he Best Of* B*lind Date* and he was even seen in a few trailers.

He was often the life and soul of parties and social occasions. At a cricket club dinner he was given a lycra onesie by guest speaker Keith Newbery. Only Phil would have put it on and headed for the dance floor.

Phil was a wild young fast bowler and, initially, found it hard to break into the team. Godshill's four principal bowlers, namely Batten, Lewis, Denness and Hannam, had combined ages of not far off 200 years. He was bemused as to how the old guys got so many wickets. Later, when he became a top fast bowler and hard-hitting batsmen, he spent a couple of years in Island senior cricket with Northwood.

As a mine host, he was perfect. None of us really expected him to develop into a shrewd businessman. During his spell at the Fighting Cocks he was popular with both his customers and staff. Phil has always been fun to be with. In past years he's made a lot of money for our EM Hospice, with mates like Nick Julian, Paul McDermott and Kevin Bennett.

Phil has been a popular member of the Shanklin and Sandown Golf Club for many years. Despite being labelled something of a sporting hypochondriac, during his early cricketing years, he went on to teach fitness with great success.

One of his greatest personal disappointments was not getting the support from Godshill residents for his proposal for a new pavilion and village hall in their Rongs Field cricket ground. More recently, Godshill have played at Rookley before amalgamating with Shanklin.

Phil Mew is one of those fun-loving guys who has an infectious personality that endears him to so many people. It's always great to be in his company.

Back to B*lind Date*. I know Phil lost but he was not too worried, as he had to get back for an important cricket match on St Helens Green the next day. If he'd won – I'm sure he would still have chosen to play cricket!

Fiona Brothers

WHATEVER HAPPENED TO FIONA BROTHERS? In the early 1980s, she was the fastest women in the world on water, with speeds of around 130mph. After being lucky to survive an horrendous powerboat crash at Bodymoor Heath, in more recent years she's become one of the most accomplished cricket scorers in the country. Her fame has spread well beyond Ventnor CC and she has actually scored for a one-day international between England and South Africa, at Lords.

Fiona is the perfect proof that a lady can multitask so much better than a man. On a typical Saturday in summer, at the Newclose cricket ground, she would continually write all the meticulous details into the scorebook, update, via her laptop, the latest score for the Ventnor website, control the huge electronic scoreboard, acknowledge the umpire's signals and answer calls from the press. No guy could cope with all that!

Fiona and her brother initially shared a class three powerboat to complete in club races in her home county of Gloucestershire. The crunch came when they both qualified as international racers. With Fiona being the faster driver, she took the boat over and in 1981 was competing in worldwide formula one races. Within no time, she was challenging for the world inshore powerboat racing world title.

During one of our interviews she told me: "I was not really a natural but I was very competitive and tried to be logical and plan things out. Most of the time it was instinct and real seat of pants driving. The boats raced so closely together but, if you were clever, you could psyche up the other drivers before the race."

Being the only woman to race in the real top flight, she took on the guys and had no fear. Many were left in her wake. In 1981 she set a new world record and held it for ten years. Even Donald Campbell's daughter, Gina, could not take it away from her.

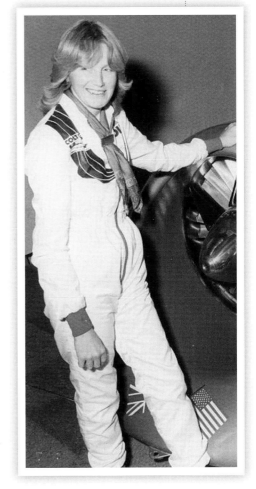

May 1983 was a month with mixed blessings. She was involved in a very bad crash and was so lucky to have even survived. Her boat touched another and flipped, went airborne into a pancake roll and crashed into the water, with her still in it. She was unconscious for 36 hours and suffered a fractured skull and serious injuries to the nerves in her face. Amazingly, she was back racing within four months but retired the following year. It was a dangerous sport, being faster than ocean powerboats, and at least six of her contemporaries lost their lives.

Fiona first scored for Ventnor Cricket Club in 1972. Actually, she scored again, when she met her late husband Keith. At the time, she was the barmaid in the nearby Garden Tavern. They met again in 1981 and married a year later. In between scoring for the club she enjoyed her powerboat years.

In latter years her day job has been in the legislation and standards department of St Mary's Hospital. Many will know her for singing in local choirs and she has also been involved with our IW Marlins Swimming Club.

Apparently, she once played a parrot in a local pantomime. She wasn't typecast, surely! I have never reminded her of this – or the time she drove the Ventnor CC minibus over her precious laptop.

CHAPTER 108

Rob 'Emu' Farley

SINCE 1971 it's been hard to avoid Rob Farley – and who would want to. Any person that instantly makes you smile is welcome at any time. Where might you have seen him? It could have been as a door knocker for Betterwear, on the road as a commercial traveller, selling sweets and tobacco, refereeing an Island football match, on stage for the Don Mills Variety Club, parading as a Rod Hull look-a-like in local carnivals, lurking as an assistant manager at the Friends of St Mary's Hospital cafe or showing you to your seat at Newport's Medina Theatre. He's been around a bit.

Rob, known locally and on the mainland as Emu, due to his resemblance to the late Rod Hull, had his own for many years, made from raffia and ladies tights. Everyone was always pleased to see it – except Rod Hull. Rob confronted him once, at an Island Motor Show, complete with his ladies tights version. It was a very brief liaison.

He was a much-loved salesman, with a quick story for every occasion.

"I treated my customers as if they were my own parents. It was all about respect but we had fun as well. You just had to sell yourself first – and then it became easier."

When he joined Booker, as a catering salesman, he was soon asked about particular meat cuts. It had been easier selling Mars bars, as he didn't know one end of the cow from the udder!

When working for Sinclair & Collis he was asked to collect money from a bad payer. Rob was quickly told to clear off, or something like that, and he left with no cash and the door handle, which had come off in his hand. Once, when he called in at Ventnor's Terminus pub, for an order, he was surprised to see Keith Fradgley, the popular local dentist, sat in there eating two bags of pork scratchings. As he left, Keith shouted out: "Keep selling the sweets. It's good for trade."

Rob, who was born in Birmingham, began football refereeing in the city and then continued when he moved to the Island. Locally, he refereed from 1972 until 2008. At one time he made the top ten of Hampshire League referees but was never likely to earn £100,000 a year officiating in the Premier League.

During one of our several interviews he told me: " I was once told I would have gone a lot further if I'd booked and sent off more players. I preferred to have a quiet word in their ear."

A year or two ago he received a special award for 50 years service to the IW Referees Association. Locally, his first-ever match was between arch enemies Brading and Seaview. The final score was Seaview 1 Brading 6. Tony Grimwade scored a hat-trick for the winners and Seaview's Nobby Nash lost a tooth.

"At the time I thought many of the players were swearing but was told 'furk it here' was a local expression."

Emu is a born storyteller and has kept locals amused for over 50 years. He's also very clever, as you're often in doubt as to whether it's fact or fiction. According to Rob, when he had his interview for a volunteer at the Medina Theatre, he was asked to walk backwards with a tray of ice creams.

Rob, thanks for all the entertainment. That Betterwear toilet brush you sold me is still working well!

CHAPTER 109

Dave Death

I REGULARLY LEAVE YARMOUTH late on a Friday night but I have never come close to a record set by Dave Death, the Island's former motor cycle king. Early in the morning he could get from Hill Place Lane to Newport, in just seven minutes. It wasn't on two wheels, either. It was in a three ton Austin lorry. Apparently, the road surfaces were better in those days. Farmers also kept their cows off the road.

I could listen to Dave for hours. I still often think of him, particularly when I run past the Longstones at Mottistone. He was born just 50 yards away, in a house with no sanitation, gas or electric. They did have a well for water. Don't forget, it was in 1925.

When he left school he worked for the world famous local author JB Priestley, at Billingham Manor – and he thought the world of his master.

"He was a magnificent man to work for and was so strong and powerful. I found this out one day when we went to work in the woods. We did sometimes have a problem with the long grass on his lawns. He would write for weeks at a time and would not allow the mower to be used, as it would disturb him. We had to get the sheep in from the farm next door."

Dave first started his motorcycle business in Yarmouth, as a part-time occupation, back in 1955. He went full time three years later and moved to Carisbrooke in 1961. Through the years the business grew and it's now both sides of the road. The mid-'70s was the golden age for motorcycles. In one month, Dave once sold 90 machines – and they all had to be put together and fitted out for the road. They had to virtually work day and night.

He loved a good burn up and the police were always looking out for him. Apparently, they only caught him once and he was not prosecuted.

"It was all different in those days and sometimes I even had a burn up with the police. I did also come off a few times," admitted Dave.

During his life he broke both arms and legs, his collar bone and assorted fingers and toes. He really was a mad brain.

Dave was a founder member of the Island's Four Aces motorcycle stunt team. They performed at local gymkhanas and open-air events. The original four were Andy Dove, Art McManus, Nip Hayles and Dave. There were no crash helmets in those days. On one occasion, he had a lucky escape. Andy Dove, a brilliant local rider, was looking for more excitement and decided the four would go through their tunnel of fire stripped to the waist. Dave revealed how lucky he was.

"I was the clown in the act and went last on my small 98cc machine. I got halfway through and there was no oxygen left, due to the fire, and the bike cut out. I had to paddle it through and got blistered all over. I never did that again. I was never really frightened but on that occasion, I did worry a bit."

He was keen to praise Andy Dove. "Andy was a superb rider and did some frightening things on his machine."

I'm sure when I was a youngster I saw Andy Dove doing the Wall of Death at a local fair.

During his eventful life some tried to call him Dave 'Dee-ath'. He wouldn't hear of it and was proud of being Dave Death. It certainly proved more of a help than a hindrance, particularly with regard to his business.

The other night I got from Hill Place Lane to Gunville in nine minutes. What a let down!

CHAPTER 110

John Woodford

WHEN I FIRST MET JOHN WOODFORD he was the catering manager at Blackgang Chine. He was very businesslike, had a good sense of humour and always found me a cup of coffee. A year or two later I had quite a shock when I saw him wearing a dress and high heels. Perhaps I ought to explain that he was actually playing dame in a pantomime. I selected him on many occasions as the Best Dame in the IW Amateur Theatre Awards.

The last time I interviewed John was just before he emerged as Dolly Dumpling in Shorwell and Grizelda in Ventnor. Whenever I see him walking down the main street in Whitwell, it's hard to imagine he's the fastest thing I've ever seen – wearing high heels. He assures me it's just for Christmas – and I believe him. There were rumours in the village that he had a garden shed full of dresses. I sneaked in for a quick look but there was not a Versace in sight – just a few old hoes and prongs.

John is a little shy in everyday life but his personality changes the minute he steps on a stage. I have seen him perform so many different roles in plays and musicals, all without a dress or high heels.

At his first school he became the teacher's favourite and was given all the solos to sing. Many years later, that same inspirational teacher, Jean Rashley, with the help of her cousin, Joy Wroath, managed to get him an audition with the highly rated Island Savoyards and he's never looked back. It had been rather different a few years earlier.

"I had wanted to join the Savoyards in the late '70s but was very shy about it. I was invited to one of their evenings but I stood outside and was too frightened to go in. It was nearly 20 years before I went back," admitted John.

He did join the Niton Drama Group, where he knew most of the people, and appeared in plays for about ten years. His character parts were so well received and the group went on to become the Pepperpot Players. When not performing, he was happy to join their front-of-stage helpers.

I loved being in a pantomime audience when members and fans of the Savoyards turned up to watch. There were always a few ad libs flying about. John used to come down into the audience for a laugh or two. I was prepared – and always hid in the back row.

John's love of performing has made it something of a family tradition. Andrew, his eldest son, had taken the lead in numerous local productions and is now a professional musical director. He's appeared at many famous theatres and on cruise liners. Jamie, his other son, is a fine drummer and has his own entertainment business. His wife, Jane, also helps out selling programmes and taking tickets.

Dave, John's late father, was also quite an entertainer himself. His lorry driver stories, live on my IW Radio chat show, were enjoyed by thousands of local people. Thankfully, Mary, his very supportive wife, also came in to keep an eye on him.

John actually spent his early years living at Knowles Farm, next to St Catherine's Lighthouse. Dad ran the farm for many years before moving back to lorry driving. John loved the remoteness of the area. In those days there were no 4x4 school runs – just the long walk to Niton Primary.

CHAPTER 111

Leslie Harvey

BACK IN THE '50s, when I left school, I had no real career plans. I was much too shy to ever dream of becoming a journalist or broadcaster. Thanks to my school sports master, Vic Read, a great early hero of mine, I finally got an interview at the Island's leading mineral water manufacturers Gould, Hibberd and Randall. Vic had a contact there. I subsequently joined the company at their Church Litten offices, now Marks and Spencer. Our donkey-in-the-well local plaque is still on the outside wall.

At that time, a gentle man called Leslie Harvey was the company manager. Being quite naive, I was always a little nervous when I went into his office. I did admire him so much and he was definitely a hands-on boss. He could be seen on the bottling plant, in the very secretive syrup room or driving the land rover along the beach to isolated summer kiosks at all hours of the day or night, depending on tides.

I was in the sales office and then went on the road as a rep. I made the mistake of leaving for a while but, thankfully, was welcomed back. Eventually I had the chance to join United Biscuits, Britain's biggest biscuit manufactures. I had gained so much more confidence in those days and really wanted the job as one of their two Island-based salesmen. The other was a wonderful man called Bert Spicer, who taught me such a lot.

I knocked on Leslie's door to seek his advice. I had been offered the job. He told me straight away that I should accept it – and he was right, of course. I stayed for 29 years until I became full time in the media.

I lost contact with Leslie. He'd retired in 1983 and eventually moved to the mainland. Gould, Hibberd and Randall's had been swallowed up by Beechams, which, sadly, was a sign of the times. Wherever possible, I still support local firms.

Imagine my surprise in 2012, when I was told 94-year old Leslie Harvey was back on the Island and living in Lake. Within a few months I'd had him on my radio show and written an article about him in *The Beacon*. What a memory, too! I got to know more about him than I ever did when I gingerly went into his office.

Leslie, who was born in Chale Green, had lived as a boy at Bridgecourt Farm, Godshill. On leaving school he trained to be an accountant. When national service came along he was given the choice of two years or he could join the Island's Princess Beatrice Rifles, who were a Territorial Army unit. He chose the latter, before being officially called up to army duty at Bouldnor.

He told me: "I worked with the defensive weapons that were placed to prevent enemy shipping coming into the Solent. We had six inch naval guns and during the trial firing, the guns slipped on the clay surface and were useless, so we left Bouldnor Battery."

Eventually, he joined the RASC and was involved with supplying the fuel for the famous Pluto Line, which ran across the Island and under the Channel en route to providing fuel for our troops in France.

In fact, Leslie went into the army as a private and came out as a captain. He joined Gould, Hibberd and Randall in 1948, as an assistant to the company secretary, and ended up as the managing director.

In 1957 their lemonade was voted the best in Britain. To celebrate, they made the Kixse name, used for their popular Wight Spice Cordial, their overall brand logo.

I still cherish memories of 11am every Christmas Day morning when mum brought in a hot glass of Kixse and shortbread biscuits. It was an Island custom.

CHAPTER 112

Roy Shiner

WHEN I WAS AT SCHOOL a guy called Roy Shiner was a hero to many of us young football fans. We had local soccer heroes like Roy Gilfillan, Ash Wingham and Joe Reed but there was so much more mystique about him – and he was an Islander. He played for Sheffield Wednesday in the old Football League First Division, now the Premiership. We just read about his goal scoring feats in our daily newspapers. There were no television cameras filming every goal – and he got 93 in 153 games for the Yorkshire club.

Locally, he'd played for East Cowes Vics and later Ryde Sports, where he got 50 goals in a season. He scored a hat-trick for Hampshire and had trials with Wolves. Top Southern League team Cheltenham Town took a chance with him and he scored 40 goals in a season and was signed by Huddersfield Town and paid £12 a week.

Roy once told me: "Huddersfield weren't too pleased when I told them I was 27. They thought I was only 24."

In four seasons he played 30 games for the club and then an amazing thing happened, back on the Island, during the summer break. A Sheffield Wednesday club scout came here for a holiday and was asked to tap him up. Yes, it happened in those days, too. Liverpool didn't invent it. Wednesday were looking for a replacement for their star striker Derek Dooley, whose tragic leg amputation had shocked a nation. Roy had played well against them.

"The deal was sorted out and I got £17 a week plus a house. In my first season I scored 33 goals in 42 games and we won promotion to the First Division," reflected Roy.

Being such a modest guy, he didn't say much about being carried off, shoulder high, and being cheered by thousands of fans. In total, he made 150 appearances for the club. His 100th goal in the Football League came against the legendary Busby Babes, at Old Trafford.

Roy revealed some of the toughest centres halves he had played against. It was not surprising that Maurice Norman, Billy Wright, Jack Charlton and Dave Ewing were high on the list.

In today's crazy world of football, youngsters join major clubs when they have barely started school. They would never look at a player aged 27. In a way, Roy was the original Jamie Vardy, a modern day exception to the rule.

Roy finished his Football League career at Hull and then went back to non-league football with Cheltenham. Eventually, he moved back to the Island with his wife, Maureen, and started his own building business. Originally, he'd worked in a local shipyard.

Always keen to put something back into the game he loved, Roy built a brilliant local team at Seaview. They won so many league and cup honours and were such a feared side. The likes of the Allen brothers, Nobby Nash and 'Dubby' Cole became local legends.

When Roy left to manage Newport, he paved the way for more local footballers to play in Hampshire League soccer at Church Litten, which, at that time, was a break from the mainland invasions of previous seasons.

When Roy died in 1988 there was a massive turn out for his funeral. He meant so much, to so many people. He was a true gentlemen and would have loved the fact that other Islanders like James Hayter, Lewis Buxton, Simon Moore, Shaun Cooper, Dan Butler, Gareth Williams and Lee Bradbury had followed him into professional football. They certainly started on more than £12 a week.

CHAPTER 113

Derek Sprake

CHALE'S DEREK SPRAKE has always been a popular character on the Island's public speaking circuit. He could talk about anything. In 1996 he made his first appearance on my radio show and was invited back. The back of the Wight smuggling stories had always fascinated me and his past family were certainly involved. Having their own brewery in the village and a fishing boat business was also rather handy. Both his father and grandfather were carriers. They never made a lot of money but it was much safer than smuggling brandy.

"My family were not so prominent as some other local names during the smuggling years. That could have been because they were never caught. Apparently, they were very generous to the community, probably for an obvious reason," said Derek.

Mind you, the local citizens of the law always knew where they could sneak a tot of brandy, if they kept quiet. Hung on the pigsty, behind the brewery, was a brandy tub and they could help themselves.

Derek then revealed a great story. "Over the years the brandy had sunk into the wood and when you added liquid it tasted even better. One night someone piddled into the tub and the local policeman was more delighted than usual, as there was more in there."

The Chale smugglers worked hard for their brandy. Sometimes, in a day, they would row across the Channel and back. Once they even took a local lady for a day out to France. Derek reckoned it was to see what her husband was up to.

In 1896, Derek's grandfather, Percy, founded their carrier business and his father continued it into the '60s.

Their regular daily trip to Newport and back, went via the villages of Chale, Atherfield and others, en route to St Thomas' Square, the hub of the Island carriers. They transported people, livestock, parcels and virtually anything else.

Derek once met a lady, who, at the age of seven, went on a holiday from East Cowes to Chale. She was left sat in St Thomas' Square for two hours, with a label around her neck, to say she was going to be called for by Sprake's carrier lorry.

Customers would put out a flag if they wanted the carrier to call. This was normally a piece of material on the end of a stick. For 20 years, one lady used the same pair of her old bloomers. I bet they weren't made in Taiwan!

Derek's father had one particular embarrassing moment. He was taking six ducks to Newport Market. They were in a cardboard box and escaped on the journey. On his way home he had to go and apologise to the customer. She told him not to worry. They were back on the lawn and would not go to market any more.

There was a great local book written by Derek, called *Put Out The Flag*. This is the story of local carriers, including his own family. It may still be available. He also came back on my show to publicise another fascinating book, *The Men Of Chale*.

When I went to Chale to plan his appearance on my show, he also had to choose some music. I was completely shocked when he told me he'd never bought a record or a CD in his life. Thankfully, he did listen to the radio and chose Cilla Black, Cliff Richard and Liza Minnelli.

Derek's latest book, *An Isle Of Wight Raconteur*, came out in early 2018.

During several interviews, I've not had the courage to tell him I'd never tried brandy. I wonder if that pigsty is still there?

CHAPTER 114

Roger Poynter

EX-ISLAND COPPER Roger Poynter has never been a name dropper but during his life he's mixed with some of the most famous people in the world. No, I don't mean some of his great old cricket mates like Mick Blackman, Alan Gurney and Keith Mitchell! More like, Muhammad Ali, Princess Diana and Lord Louis Mountbatten.

I enjoy Roger's company and never tire of his stories. A great competitor, as many found out when they played cricket against him and the all-conquering Newport team. They could have easily held their own in today's Southern League Premier Division. At this point, I want to leave Roger's cricket exploits.

Roger regularly drove the Royals on their visits to the Island. Lord Louis Mountbatten was a particular favourite and our Governor was full of surprises, as well as being a stickler for time.

On one occasion, they were early for an engagement at Carisbrooke Castle and Lord Louis suggested they parked the car and went for a walk. They were seen strolling up Betty Haunt Lane. Roger once turned up at the Royal Yacht Squadron and found him asleep. He had an engagement in Shanklin. When they got to Northwood Garage, the Governor realised he'd left his speech at the Squadron. Suddenly, time was of the essence, especially when they got stuck behind a cement mixer. For a few miles Roger became a Stirling Moss drive-a-like and just about made the finishing line. They were late and Roger got the blame from a special branch officer.

Driving Princess Diana on May 30, 1985, was an occasion he'll never forget. The day before, they'd borrowed a funeral car for the visit and Roger noticed a particular smell and quickly put some scent cards in. The following morning, just after he took them out, the police dog jumped in the back seat with dirty paws. Another hasty clean-up was required.

"When I was driving Diana, she said to me 'If I didn't know any better, I would think this is an undertaker's vehicle.' When we got to Sandown Airport she broke away from the dignitaries to personally thank me for driving her for the day. I had a police superintendent stood nearby and he asked me what she'd said. I told him it was a private conversation and wouldn't tell him."

When Roger was waiting to drive the Duchess of Kent from Seaclose to the Earl Mountbatten Hospice, he managed to split the seam of his trousers, right down the crutch. He quickly arranged for a colleague to go to his house and get another suit. At the hospice, he was initially barred from the Royal toilet, until he explained the reason he needed it to change in.

Roger didn't think the Duchess had noticed. Her detective certainly had. Wearing his black suit, her driver denied he'd had a green one on earlier. In the end, he did reveal the truth. If he hadn't changed the suit – even more might have been revealed!

The personal highlight of his career was at Arsenal's Highbury Stadium, when he was in the Metropolitan Police. It was at the 1966 Muhammad Ali fight with Henry Cooper. He was in the escort party for the American boxing legend and spent some time alone with him in the dressing room.

Roger told this story on my radio and TV shows.

"I had never seen a physique like it. He had muscles where I never knew they existed and he did the Ali shuffle in front of the full length mirror. He said to me 'Aren't I just the greatest heavyweight you've ever seen?' I just couldn't believe it – and he was."

CHAPTER 115

John Hayward

I FIRST MET JOHN HAYWARD when he played cricket for Porchfield. Their pitch, a farmer's field with a wicket cut in the middle of it, was very sporting, particularly to bowlers. On one occasion I played there we were out for 20 runs – and still won the game. The village team made just 18. On that memorable day they didn't even have time to slow us down a bit in the tea interval with huge cakes and sandwiches. It was always a social occasion, with the Sportsmen's Rest just down the road.

John was such a gentle man and brought a real genial touch to his endless fund of stories. The family had been at Little Thorness Farm since 1919 and John's grandfather had paid just £2000 for the 100 acres.

In the Second World War ten men were stationed on the farm to man the searchlight and John remembered it vividly.

"They used our farm to practise commando landings and tanks came in off the landing craft. The public were banned from the beach and the troops often built trenches into the cliffs, covered by tin. We also had to be careful when harvesting because they had things all over the place."

John could never forget the day the bay was filled with small boats and troops in preparation for the D-Day landings. It seemed there were giant upturned tables floating everywhere. These turned out to be the caissons used to form the famous Mulberry Harbour.

"When we got up the next day, which was June 3, they had all gone. We knew something was up because there was a double guard on the searchlight."

One Boxing Day, just before the end of the war, the troops cleared off to the pub and left John and a neighbour, Bill Abrook, in charge of the searchlight.

John recalled that day. "We started the engine and if anything had come over we would have just followed other beams but there had not been a raid for some time."

He actually took over the family farm and milk round in 1964 and loved being a trusted servant to the Northwood community. He signed adoption and will forms and saw families grow up. Many gave him door keys to put the milk in the fridge while they were at work. For some older people he was their daily contact with the outside world. On one occasion, he saved the life of a lady who could have died in a fire. True to form, John never wanted to say much about that. He was such a modest man.

What of those days? John told me: "The '60s and '70s were the great days for the milk rounds. Then the supermarkets came along to spoil it all. Now the milk producers get a raw deal and are well underpaid for the work they put in. I can remember over 300 milk producers on the Island. Now it's less than 30."

Even when his son Nigel took over the farm, John was happy to stand in on the milk round and help with the haymaking.

Many still remember John for his 40 years at Porchfield Cricket Club.

"I started batting at number 11 and worked my up to number one. When I got back to number 11 again, I gave up the game."

I had the thrill of taking a cricket team of *Weekly Post* Sports Personalities to open their brand new ground. This one favoured the batsmen.

CHAPTER 116

John Hilsum

IN THE EARLY '70s, if Brighstone Cricket Club had welcomed John Hilsum to their club, when he first arrived on the Island, he might not have become such a legend in local cricket circles. As he wasn't living in the village, they were not too keen. He joined Ventnor instead and changed the face of Island cricket.

Ironically, I am writing this chapter just after seeing Travis Head play for Australia against England. John loved watching him during his one season with Ventnor. I'm sure John's credibility and popularity within Southern League cricket must have helped Head's placement with the Island club. Sadly, John died much too young, in 2016, and the Ventnor church was packed and people came from all over England to celebrate his life.

I loved playing against John. He was a fierce competitor on the field but such a genial and gentle man, without his whites on. He was a fascinating guy to talk to and, to me, his conversations were a kind of therapy. When I first interviewed him, in 1977, he was more keen to talk about other people than himself. At the time he was the captain of both Ventnor and the Isle of Wight representative team. With a jug of beer to sip at, John did reveal a little about himself.

Apparently, his love of cricket was due to a couple of spinsters from a village school near Winchester. Sensing his enthusiasm for the game they encouraged him as much as they could. When the captain of Northwood stayed with them for a few days, John received his first real coaching.

John played village cricket at the age of ten for Hinton Ampner. Their ground was on a hill and a favourite spot for many of the local girls, as they had no pavilion and had to change in the open. He batted at number 11 and fielded at fine leg.

Later, when he went to Alresford Secondary Modern, he played for Hampshire Schools. He also played for King Alfred's College in Winchester and Petersfield. When he became a schoolteacher he was keen to increase the pupils interest in the game. This

was later highlighted when he was so influential in starting the Ventnor Cricket Academy.

In March 1972, when John looked over the wall at Steephill, he saw the Ventnor pavilion. By the time he joined them in August, they didn't have one. Being a craft teacher he was signed as the chief chippy in the building of their new clubhouse. On the field, he had great success and scored over 1000 runs in a season on three occasions.

John told me: "We seem to attract players who care about the club and anyone who comes must have this. On winter Sunday mornings players are always keen to improve the facilities."

He helped to make Ventnor a force again. In 1993, as club chairman, he led the club into the Hampshire League. It took many promotions but they made the Southern League Gold Division in 2010. John was the driving force behind the £1.1 million pavilion and coaching centre.

I was delighted to be invited to the ceremony in 2017 when Ventnor renamed their pavilion, The John Hilsum Pavilion. A much deserved honour and his name will live on for as long as they play cricket at Ventnor.

So many of us were thrilled when John was given the British Empire Medal for services to cricket and the community. He was also inducted into the Paul Harris Fellowship, for his work with Ventnor Rotary Club.

CHAPTER 117

David White

I HAVE SO MUCH to thank David White for. This local photographer personally arranged my interview with Hollywood icon Charlton Heston. Chuck is probably the most famous person I've ever interviewed. That was in 1999 and two years earlier, David had been a guest on my radio chat show.

He was a personal friend of the late Charlton Heston and had tipped me off about Charlton's visit to his wife's photographic exhibition, at Freshwater's Dimbola Lodge. I'd already interviewed Lydia Heston at this exhibition.

Two weeks after Charlton's visit, David rang me to see how my interview had gone. I had to explain he'd been running late and there had been no time for a proper interview. He'd just managed a few quotes and sound bites for the south coast media.

David told me Charlton and Lydia were coming back to England to do a two-handed play in the West End and he would sort me out an interview. There was a happy ending. I ended up interviewing Charlton in a posh London hotel. It was much more than a two minute news interview for a radio station. In fact, I spoke to him for just over an hour.

When David came on my show it was just a couple of months after he'd returned from an amazing trip, with his cameras of course, to the Amazon Rain Forest. He had some stories just bursting to get out.

One day he was sat alongside the pilot in a small Cessna plane that became surrounded in mist. It suddenly cleared and the wing tip was just 10 feet from a mountain. He also found the wreckage of a crashed Dakota that went down in the dense jungle back in the 1940s – and even brought back a piece of metal from it. The Indians had taken all the seats out but it was still clearly visible as a plane.

On another occasion, their canoe overshot the rapids. After the drop, the bow went under and, luckily, came up again. They got very wet and David lost a camera. He also became the first European to record a particular Indian tribe singing and dancing, which we played on-air. They'd had little contact with the outside world.

"We also had a real problem crossing a flooded Amazon river. The Indians made us a raft but it was washed away in the flowing waters. I suggested we go further down the river to try and find a crossing point – and we did. I was not a good swimmer, although I told them I was, and could have been swept away at any time.

"We all signed a pact to say that none of us would hold each other responsible, in case they didn't make it," said David.

After five days in the jungle, David came into a village unshaven, dishevelled and wearing a khaki shirt and bush hat. He met two Indians from a tribe who had no contact with the Western World or radio and television. He was amazed at their subsequent comment: "Wow – Indiana Jones."

On the Island, David has taken photos of Ringo Starr, Billy Fury, Simon Le Bon, the Yorkshire Ripper and Jeremy Thorpe, who was cuddling a donkey. Some of these went all around the world. Lord Louis Mountbatten also allowed him to take a portrait.

David's worked for *The Times*, *Daily Mirror*, *Daily Mail*, *Daily Telegraph*, *the County Press*, and the *Wight Life* magazine. Once he had the main front page picture on the *Sunday Mirror*. He might even have photographed your local wedding.

CHAPTER 118

Henry Adams

OUR HENRY HAS A GREAT STORY and if you need cheering up – he's the guy. His life includes being a trainer for racing turtles, selling wet fish, being a lifetime supporter of Pompey, setting a round the Island rowing record, selling local bananas in his open-all-hours shop, refusing an entry to Jimi Hendrix at the Afton Pop Festival and being abused by some members of the Ryde Conserative Club for taking a Liberal friend for a drink. Despite all this, he achieved the ultimate accolade from his own home town by becoming the Mayor of Ryde. Well done, your worship.

You could probably write a complete book on Henry Adams. It's all happened to him and, thankfully, he fought back from a serious illness. We've had a few laughs over the years. I love the story of how the local sign on the tomatoes outside of Henry's Ryde shop blew on to the bananas. Initially, he was unaware but surprised when visitors kept coming in for his local bananas. One coach party, who returned the next year, even came back for some more of his Isle of Wight bananas.

When Henry worked for MacFisheries they gave him a few days off to work at the 1970 Pop Festival. He could put his hand to anything – like guarding the septic tank and checking the artists, as they came into their special area.

"I was on the gate and this curly haired geezer came in with no badge. I told him he couldn't go in. He told me his name was Jimi Hendrix but I said that made no difference. I said to him, to prove you are, sign this bit of paper for me – and he did," said Henry. He kept it and years later sent it to a London auction with a reserve price of £2000.

His first-ever job was working as a bellboy and comi waiter on Cunard liners. On the SS *Franconia* he became their turtle trainer. The passengers were even told he'd been trained by the London Zoological Society.

"There was a tote and most of the races were won by a three-legged turtle. The band, of course, knew this and often cleaned up. There was I, at just over 16, being introduced to backhanders from the musicians."

When he came back to the Island he became a trainee manager for MacFisheries. He had a work van but no-one would get in it for a ride home from the Ryde Rowing Club. They liked 'Fishy' Adams but not the smell.

Henry has been at the club for over 60 years. Initially, he was just an enthusiastic rower. Since then he's taken many different roles and has also been an official of the Hants and Dorset Amateur Rowing Association.

"When I was rowing I sometimes had a bout of gastroenteritis on a Friday night and could not go to work on the Saturday. Then I got rumbled, when the manager saw my name in the *County Press*. I told him I'd got better quickly and was well enough to travel to Bournemouth. In the end, I had to make a choice and I chose rowing."

He also became a postman but didn't like getting up early. After a good night at Yelf's, he would get in at midnight and have to be at work four hours later.

When Henry appeared on my TV chat show I surprised him by wearing a Pompey shirt. He loved it but called me an "old scummer." I had no idea what he meant!

CHAPTER 119

Sheila Hancock

EARLY IN 1984, Sheila Hancock, who was born in Blackgang, was due to come back home as the tour director of the Royal Shakespeare Company. In November of the previous year, we'd agreed to meet in the foyer of Broadcasting House. This was for a *Weekly Post* article and she would come to me directly after a major radio interview. She kept her promise but was en route to Derby and could spare me just five minutes. Somehow, I got enough to fill a page but had little time to talk about the Island.

This changed 25 years later when we met again. This time at Portsmouth University, where she was the Chancellor, and she was not in a hurry.

In the early '30s her father was the manager of the Blackgang Hotel.

"I can remember it was a very small hotel in those days and we had a skeleton of a whale in our back garden. I was surprised when I came back a few years ago with my husband John (Thaw). We had a picnic and it seemed more like a fairground."

In her best-selling book, *The Two Of Us*, she had written: "My parents told me tales of smugglers and incest in that cut-off part of the Island."

Sheila had told me on our first meeting that she had heard rumours of other things that took place at Blackgang – or perhaps, came off, might have been more appropriate! Her family left the Island when her father was moved to the mainland by his employers, Brakspear Beers.

During the early part of her acting career she spent three years with the resident Barry O'Brien Repertory Company at Shanklin Theatre. They were wild summers and their off stage antics did not always impress the local dignitaries. They also suggested the on stage love scenes should be less passionate.

"The watch committee of Shanklin even complained that I had been seen walking in the main street wearing brief shorts and it was not to happen again. It was all so different in those days. Any guns in the pictures outside of the theatre were taped out and no kissing or underwear photos were allowed," said Sheila.

During those early summers in Shanklin, Sheila was wooed by the leading man, Alec Ross. Any romantic scenes they had on stage must have been carefully monitored. Mind you, there are a lot of hideaway rooms in Shanklin Theatre! Eventually, they married and came back as husband and wife.

For one summer Sheila left the more legitimate stage to join Cyril Fletcher's *Summer Masquerade*, at Sandown Pier Pavilion. They had several changes of programme and she found it hard to adapt. On one occasion, unfortunately, she came on as an Indian squaw in a cockney scene. Those Island summer seasons and other touring shows at Ryde Pavilion gave her such invaluable experience and equipped her for later stardom. Television's *The Rag Trade* helped to make her one of Britain's favourite actors.

In her fantastic career she's made 40 movies, played the original Miss Hannigan in the West End's *Annie* and won an Olivier Award for her London appearance in the musical *Cabaret*. In more recent years she guested in *New Tricks* and *Grumpy Old Women*. She was also Barbara Owen in *EastEnders*.

Sheila Hancock has always been a real fighter. She has lost two husbands with cancer and also recovered from her own breast cancer.

CHAPTER 120

Bill Brett

IN MY TEENS, when I began playing cricket for East Cowes, I had heard of the infamous Brett brothers from Westover Park Cricket Club, the team that played out in the wilds on a pitch that was either the first or second turning on the left, past the road junction to Newbridge. Playing them was a daunting task and they had some wonderful players,

including Bill, his brother John and the Porter brothers. Not surprisingly, they lost few games in their farmer's field. Sometimes they even had to chase the cows off the pitch.

Years after the wily old Bill Brett had cleverly talked some of us out, we became good friends and I enjoyed my visits to his unconventional village home. On one memorable occasion, I took a tape recorder and recorded an amazing interview for my radio show.

Bill lived in the old school and in his former classroom he had so much memorabilia (junk to his wife June). The Daily Mail did a full page spread on his treasures. It contained his old desk, the bike used by the old local nit nurse, motor cycles, dinosaur bones, a double toilet seat, his old 1933 school writing book and a sign advertising 12 bottles of beer for 3/6d

On one occasion I was looking for an old Russ Conway single. It didn't take long to find one. It was scratched, of course. Bill even found me an empty Kixse gold medal lemonade bottle, with the old label still attached. He gave it to me as a souvenir of my first job, at the mineral water manufactures, previously mentioned in the Leslie Harvey chapter.

When I was dragged to the Bank Holiday antique fairs in Calbourne I could always be found in Bill Brett's garden listening to his stories. I could hide for quite a while, as it always seemed to be overgrown.

I never tired of Bill's yarn of how he met his wife. He came out of the Horse and Groom pub at Ningwood, just as two local gals went by on bicycles. Apparently, they were looking for boys. He took a real fancy to one of them and struck gold when he chose June. I was never quite sure if she saw it quite like that! It was not a whirlwind romance and wedding bells were not imminent. In fact, they were 14 years away.

He had an excuse, of course. "I wanted to wait until I was in my 30s and had a house of my own."

Bill was actually born in Hulverstone but moved to Calbourne when he was seven. He only ever left the village to play cricket or visit a favourite country pub. His early working life began on a Calbourne farm, where he became a bit of a legend, as a rabbit catcher. Apparently, he used a ferret, which he kept in his pocket, and a wire snare.

The Brett brothers also ran a successful building firm for many years. On one occasion, the church had a bad leak, with water coming through the walls. John was ill at the time, so Bill enlisted June to help out. In the end she had to lower him down from the top of the building on a rope. Once, when Bill wasn't listening, she told me a certain thought had crossed her mind, while he was dangling on the end of the rope.

On the cricket field he never wore batting gloves. We talked about this one day and suddenly I sensed a funny line was looming. With a glint in his eye he told me: "There was another piece of protection gear I never wore. What was the use? I had nothing to put in it." I had no idea what he meant!

CHAPTER 121

And finally...
Isle of Wight Radio

WHEN ISLE OF WIGHT RADIO went on air in 1990, I was told by the two bosses, Steve Oates and Jean Paul Hansford, that they wanted me to have a chat show. I did begin to worry, as I didn't get an invite to the official Sunday opening and my picture was not in the launch brochure. It seems ironic now, as I'm the only one still there who actually began in the first week.

Steve Oates

I had little time to prepare my first show. I was told on the Thursday that I had a programme on Saturday night. Steve Oates handed over the last hour of his show for me to bring in live guests. It was scary but I managed to persuade Bernie Cullen and Island impresario, Peter Brennen, to come in live from 9pm until 10pm. It worked out so well, despite the last minute notification. Within a week or two I was given my own Saturday night slot, as *John Hannam Meets*. Amazingly, it proved very popular. Early live guests included Les Dennis, Reginald Marsh and Celia Imrie. To start 1991, I was promoted to a Sunday lunchtime slot. I have so many happy memories of the show that ran until early 2016. Now I have podcasts, via the IW Radio and my own websites plus others like Spotify and iTunes. For the first few years I had to pay my own travel expenses for mainland interviews and was a thousand or two out of pocket.

Norman Wisdom came in and I let him read the weather. It was the longest forecast ever – and had everything from snow to a heat wave. Jethro came in on the same show as Kenny Baker, R2D2. Kenny came back a few months later to surprise me but couldn't get in, as the bell was too high for him to reach. Bandleader Ray McVay came over from the mainland and arrived as I read the weather. Ruby Murray was so nervous, she held my arm for the whole show. I turned up one Sunday and found my live guests, the Bay City Rollers and Toyah Wilcox, had arrived early and were playing football outside the studio. My Cliff Richard interview drew listeners from all along the south coast. I had

John Hannam in the studio

impressionist Mike Osman in live and he took off Lawrie McMenemy. Unbeknown to him, I got Laurie to ring him up, on-air, and complain. It worked like a dream. Once, my interview with Bad Boys Inc, a popular boy band, was filmed for Japanese television.

Top comedian Charlie Williams was a frequent visitor to the Island. One Sunday, while he was staying with personal friends in Brading, he agreed to do my show live. He was staying in a house on the high mall as you come into the town from Morton Common. He was stood on a wall and I couldn't see him at all. I went around the block a few times before I finally found him. He told me that he'd seen me drive past a few times. It had gone 12-30 and we were live on-air at 1pm. Charlie held on tight – and we just made it.

And Finally... Isle of Wight Radio

One young programme controller thought my show was not really suitable for a Sunday lunchtime, so I was moved to a Sunday night. I said nothing – but went out and got interviews with Hollywood stars Charlton Heston and John Mills. It was soon back to Sunday lunchtime.

Charlton Heston

John Mills

In the early years, Jean Paul Hansford would personally write to presenters to praise their shows. That felt so rewarding. Later, Andy Shier also always went out of his way to pat you on the back.

Charlie Brook

I was asked to cover a local football match every Saturday and some evenings. I was not given any initial instructions. I was just told to go to a match and phone in goal flashes and half-time and full-time reports. It was quite daunting and my first match was on Saturday April 21, 1990. It was East Cowes Vics v Totton. Jean Paul was listening and quickly sent congratulations. I loved those days and on one memorable Saturday, I caught the 4am ferry to Portsmouth, drove to Cardiff to pick up my son from university and drove back to the Island and still made the 3pm kick-off at Whippingham.

I loved it when some of our presenters like Charlie Brook, Bill Padley, Louise Whitefield and Richard Pocock (now Rick Jackson), Chris Browning, Andy Shier and Tom Stroud moved on to further their careers. Many years earlier, a young kid from Shanklin had written to me at the Weekly Post – to tell me how good a DJ he was. Later he joined IW Radio. His name was Alex Dyke – and he's become famous along the south coast. I gave him his first-ever newspaper feature. I've now been on his Radio Solent show a few times.

Rick Jackson

Chris Browning

Pat Norris did such a lot in helping to form the Island's own radio station and he hosted a brilliant Sunday night programme called *The Garden Isle*, which was a unique show. It was such a hit and people drove all around the Island for a location game they played every week.

Andy Shier

And Finally... Isle of Wight Radio

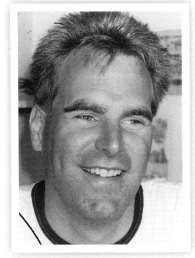

Alex Dyke

When we held our 25th anniversary party there were only two originals left – our head of sales, the lovely Sue Hudson, we had previously worked together on the *Weekly Post*, and yours truly. When we were called up to receive special 25th anniversary trays, I lost it completely. I was stunned at the honour and burst into tears, as I blubbered my way through an impromptu thank you speech. That set Sue off, and we shed our tears together.

I would personally like to thank Claire Willis and the radio staff who were around in 2006, when my wife died. They were such a comfort at a very sad time.

I would like to thank everyone I've ever worked with doing my long career at the radio station.

Claire Willis

John with Sue Hudson and their 25th Anniversary trays

Danny Briggs

Lee Probert

Rose & Graham Daish

1967 East Cowes Saro team – includes John (back row 3rd from left),
Les Snow (back row 5th from left) and Mike Greenwood (front row 2nd from left)